DIVORCING *Marriage*

DIVORCING *Marriage*

Unveiling the Dangers in Canada's New Social Experiment

Daniel Cere and Douglas Farrow, Editors

Foreword by Maggie Gallagher

Published for the Institute for the
Study of Marriage, Law and Culture
by
McGill-Queen's University Press
Montreal & Kingston • London • Ithaca

ISBN 0-7735-2894-6 (cloth)
ISBN 0-7735-2895-4 (paper)

Legal deposit third quarter 2004
Bibliothèque nationale du Québec

Printed in Canada on acid-free paper

McGill-Queen's University Press acknowledges the support of the Canada Council for the Arts for our publishing program. We also acknowledge the financial support of the Government of Canada through the Book Publishing Industry Development Program (BPIDP) for our publishing activities.

Library and Archives Canada Cataloguing in Publication

Divorcing marriage : unveiling the dangers in Canada's new social experiment / edited by Daniel Cere and Douglas Farrow.

Includes bibliographical references and index.
ISBN 0-7735-2894-6 (bnd)
ISBN 0-7735-2895-4 (pbk)

1. Same-sex marriage – Canada.   2. Same-sex marriage – Law and legislation – Canada.   I. Cere, Daniel   II. Farrow, Douglas, 1953–
III. Institute for the Study of Marriage, Law and Culture

HQ560.D59 2004   306.84'8'0971   C2004-904198-3

Index by Gillian Watts, Word Watch Editorial Services
Interior design and typesetting by Daniel Crack, Kinetics Design

Contents

Foreword

Maggie Gallagher

What message is today's push for same-sex marriage sending to our young people? I caught a glimpse recently while taking the shuttle from Washington, D.C., to my home in New York. The young man sitting next to me, a university student, was also heading home, on a break from school. Call him Matthew. We got to talking about the whole same-sex marriage thing. I must have declared my position pretty quickly, because Matthew soon asked me, "Why are you against it?"

Marriage is the place where we not only tolerate people having babies and rearing children, we positively welcome and encourage it, I told him. Same-sex marriage will be, in effect, a public and legal declaration by governments that children do not need mothers and fathers. That alternative family forms are not only just as good, they are just the same as a husband and wife bringing kids up together.

It was my turn to ask a question. "Don't you think that kids need a mom and a dad?"

"Not really," Matthew said. "I don't think so."

He told me he knew some kids at school who were being brought up by a same-sex couple. They seemed okay to him. Besides, he said, his own mom and dad were divorced. His older brother seemed to have some problems with the divorce, he hinted, but that was probably just because his brother was older and knew their dad better than he did before the divorce.

"Kids just accept whatever their family situation is. It doesn't matter," Matthew said. After all, he had grown up with a single mom and was doing just fine.

It was clear that he was doing fine, in many ways. But then I pulled out my big gun: "What about you?" I asked him. "Do you think you'll matter to your kids?"

Matthew seemed taken aback by the question. It was obvious he had never looked at it from that perspective. He thought for a moment but then followed his train of thought to the only logical conclusion he could – a train wreck: "No," he said. "Not really."

Abandon your kids early enough, he implied, and fatherlessness is all they know. They won't need you. Kids adjust.

This, of course, has been the central message of the family diversity crowd since the dawn of the sexual revolution. Adults have awesome intimacy needs that must be met. Family forms, social norms, household arrangements must be unwound and rewound so that the adults get what they need. Kids? Oh, they adjust.

One of the many ways in which same- and opposite-sex couples differ is on this thing called babies. Gays and lesbians can get children only after an enormous amount of thought and effort: through adoption, buying a baby from a woman (a.k.a. "surrogate motherhood"), or via artificial insemination. Babies don't just suddenly appear. By contrast, any of the things that men and women must do to make sure they do *not* have children outside of marriage are difficult: abstain from sex, have a shotgun wedding, use contraception consistently, or have an abortion (in descending order of moral pulchritude, in my opinion). The question is how we can rear young men and women to avoid unmarried child-bearing when our laws are saying what same-sex marriage says: that children don't need mothers and fathers – alternative family structures are just as good; that boys don't need the love of fathers – never mind the overwhelming evidence that young men reared to believe that fathers don't matter to their children do not become dependable husbands and fathers themselves.

Marriage is our most basic social institution for protecting children. Same-sex marriage amounts to a vast social experiment on children. Rewriting the basic rules of marriage puts all children, not just the children in unisex unions, at risk. Do not expect boys to become good family men in a society of Matthews who believe, as they have been taught, that men are optional in family life.

Some advocates of gay marriage are trying to persuade us that same-sex marriage won't affect marriage in general, or will even make marriage better: more tolerant and compassionate. Others argue that it won't affect anyone but the handful of gay and lesbian families. Don't believe it. The Matthews of this world have already absorbed the message of same-sex marriage very well: Fathers are optional. Adults are fragile, and their emotional needs come first. Children are resilient.

We Americans are looking northward with great interest, to a country that is seemingly moving even faster than ours down the road to the redefinition of marriage. While there are many differences between our countries, two major similarities between us on this issue stand out, to me at least. The first is that the majority of people in both of our nations are showing in opinion polls that they are increasingly *against* same-sex marriage. What has influenced them? I believe it is that they looked at the future and did not like what they saw regarding the consequences of redefining marriage: the severing of children from the protections of marriage, the stigmatization of the majority of our populations as anti-equality and anti-freedom, the increasing control of personal and social life by government, and the evisceration of education and religion by courts eager to open society up to the power politics of groups bent on creating rights, and legitimacy, for themselves.

The second similarity is that this clear signal that we do not want marriage to be redefined is not causing the slightest flutter of concern on the brows of those in the courts, lobby groups, and media who are promoting this new social experiment, so convinced are they of the rightness of their cause.

In both countries, the courts and these groups seem to be on a frolic of their own. However, in the United States, there are signs that votes may make the difference. Consider, for example, the special election for state senator in Massachusetts in March 2004. Cheryl Jacques was vacating her seat to become president and executive director of the Human Rights Campaign, a lobby for lesbian, gay, bisexual, and transgender equal rights. Jacques wanted a trusted lieutenant to take over her seat. Yet even in a safe Democratic district in an overwhelmingly liberal state, the race was close, and voters crossed party lines to elect the Republican.

In addition, the campaign to amend the U.S. Constitution to prevent the redefinition of marriage is gaining in strength, as is a similar campaign in Canada.

I do not know whether the political structures in Canada will be able to offset the judicial. I do not know whether the people of Canada will make their wills known and felt on this issue beyond the opinion polls to the political polls. I do know that the history, experience, meaning, and institution of marriage are similar in both countries. I can only hope – we in the U.S. can only hope – that a book such as this one, which examines all these issues and more in a reasonable and compelling way, will help throw a decisive counter-punch at this new social experiment on both sides of the border.

We should not be naïve. We have a lot to lose, and so do our children. After all, doesn't the next generation of Matthews have the right to know *us* as their mothers and fathers – as a generation who cared for them, and fought for them, when it really mattered?

Acknowledgements

We would like to thank the authors for their hard work and patience during the sometimes complex process of drafting and revising the essays. We are grateful for their courage and creativity, characteristics that are always required in the struggle to widen public debate on controversial questions.

The process that led to this volume included a number of consultations and colloquia with scholars from universities and think-tanks across North America and abroad. To those who gave generously of their time, and to those who helped to organize and to fund that process, we are also very grateful. Only the individual authors, of course, are responsible for the views here expressed.

Donald G. Bastian's many contributions throughout the publication process were vital. We owe Don a special debt of gratitude for his editorial advice, good counsel, and diplomacy. To the publishers, who share in the courage and creativity of the authors by way of their dedication to the integrity of public discourse, we likewise express our thanks, and particularly to Philip Cercone.

Margaret Somerville's essay is revised from an earlier French version published in the collection of texts edited by Guy Ménard: *Mariage homosexuel: les termes du débat* (Montréal: Liber, Le Devoir, Collection: Éthique publique, 2003). The essay by Katherine K. Young and Paul Nathanson has some elements in common with their contribution to the collection *Sex, Marriage, and Family in World Religions*, Don S. Browning, M. Christian Green, and John Witte, Jr., eds. (Columbia University Press, forthcoming).

Daniel Cere and Douglas Farrow

DIVORCING *Marriage*

Canada's Romantic Mistake

Douglas Farrow

> And if it was the duty of
> married people to love each other,
> was it not equally the duty of lovers to
> marry each other and nobody else?
>
> *– Friedrich Engels*

The title of this book is *Divorcing Marriage*, by which is meant, in the first instance at least, something like what Justice Blair meant when he spoke of the profound change in the law on which his court had decided. For that court – the original *Halpern* court of 2002, which was the first to mandate same-sex marriage – had determined to do the necessary thing. It had determined to divorce marriage from procreation. Our title, however, has a further and more contentious meaning. By it we intend to make obvious what the *Halpern* court tried to obscure, namely, that what is now to be called marriage is not at all the same thing as what used to be called marriage. What used to be called marriage is being set aside together with procreation. It, too, is being divorced.

In charitable moments, when less conscious of the acrimonious and litigious nature of the divorce, I like to think of this as Canada's romantic mistake. For the process on which our country has embarked – that of exchanging marriage as it has always been known for marriage as it has never been known – is guided by a romantic outlook in at least three ways.

First, it is guided by the romantic equation of love and marriage, captured in the 1955 Sammy Cahn song popularized by Frank Sinatra. You can try to separate them, wrote Cahn, but that's just an illusion:

> *Love and marriage, love and marriage,*
> *Go together like a horse and carriage.*
> *Dad was told by mother . . .*
> *You can't have one without the other.*[1]

It is not so far as it seems from 1955 to 2002. To be sure, in 1955 few would have said that the reference to dad and mother, and with it the implied link between marriage and procreation, was entirely dispensable to the concept of marriage. But in the intervening years we have learned how to follow the logic of Cahn's equation. If marriage is essentially about a couple's love, and if not all loving couples are opposite-sex couples, then marriage need not necessarily be restricted to a man and a woman, or point to a mom and a dad. This simple logic makes good use of another set of Cahn lyrics: "From this lovely rainbow we're riding free / Love makes us whatever we want to be." Or maybe we should say, appealing to a rather older tradition fostered by Friedrich Engels, that love makes marriage whatever we want it to be.[2]

The second way in which Canada's adventure with same-sex marriage is guided by a romantic outlook takes us one decade farther along, to the civil-rights movement of the 1960s. By itself, the romantic logic (marriage = love, hence love mandates marriage) would never have led to a court order for same-sex marriage licences. This required another kind of logic, the logic of rights. What we used to call marriage stipulates a union between a man and a woman. But that stipulation, by excluding same-sex couples, reinforces inequality. The exclusion, therefore, must be overruled in a society committed to equality. Nothing romantic here, surely; just hard logic in the service of justice. But isn't it nice to know that in following this logic we are walking in the footsteps of Martin Luther King, Jr., and of his brothers and sisters in the civil-rights movement? The struggle for gay marriage, like the struggle against the anti-miscegenation laws of America's southern states, is a noble one that keeps alive the heroic spirit of the freedom marches. (Is that not what justifies the pictures we saw in the papers of *Halpern* judges celebrating their landmark decision over drinks, arm in arm with activists and former litigants?) The march toward freedom is still moving. The old are still young, and the only question is where to march next.

The third way in which Canada's experiment with same-sex marriage is romantic in outlook is not quite so obvious. It is equally important, however. I am speaking of the motivating virtue of "tolerance," always the first and the last word in any debate about same-sex marriage or gay rights generally. Arguments about the rightness or wrongness of replacing the age-old definition of marriage with a gender-neutral definition may, or may not, be made with clarity in courts of law. But in the media, in Parliament, and in most public discourse these arguments are rarely conducted with the patience required to measure what is right or wrong, sound or unsound. Patience is not the virtue required. "All you need is love" – or, rather, all *they* need is love, and all *you* need is tolerance. For tolerance is the virtue of virtues in our society. It is the one thing necessary for a society that dares to call itself free, and civil. This, too, is a form of romanticism, if not of utopianism. It is a form with roots in the historic Romantic movement, in the Enlightenment, and especially in Rousseau. But today's romanticism is not nearly so sophisticated as all that. It is the naïve kind of romanticism that comes very close to thinking that "love is always right" and that society can be run on tolerance alone. So long, that is, as we remember at least this much of Rousseau: that we must be resolutely intolerant of anything we deem to be intolerance!

These diverse but powerful romantic elements in the consciousness of Canadians mean that the divorce process, however acrimonious while it lasts, cannot last long. Indeed, it appears almost to be over before it has even begun. In the matter of marriage, if our courts have their way, Canadian law will soon be wedded to a new partner: same-sex marriage.

I called this Canada's romantic *mistake*, and so it is. The book's subtitle rightly warns of perils on the path our nation is walking. It is the business of the following essays to point out some of those perils, and to show where mistakes have been made. One such mistake can already be mentioned here, namely, a refusal to think clearly about actions and consequences. Our readers will find in what follows an invitation to pause for thought before plunging ahead with this new adventure, the adventure with marriage that is not marriage. They will find nothing against romance in these pages, much less against love! They are forewarned, however, that they will find much to disabuse them of the threefold romantic outlook referred to above.

Few people in Canada understand the dynamics of the marriage debate better than Daniel Cere; no one, perhaps, has followed it more closely on both sides of the border. His opening reflections provide an opportunity to begin questioning the first form of our romantic outlook, by considering the way in which the "pure-love" or "couple-centred" model of marriage has come to compete with the traditional model. (Here we discover that the new and profoundly different thing being proposed has a longer and less savoury family history than we may have imagined.) John McKay also offers an account of that competition and of the conflict it has created, from his perspective as a member of the Justice Committee that held hearings on the subject.

The three subsequent essays are equally sobering in their exploration of the consequences of adopting the new model that divorces marriage from procreation. They point directly and indirectly to some of the dangers in the hasty social experiment that Canada is about to undertake. The authors of these essays include ethicists, lawyers, historians, and religion- and culture-critics. (The controversial Margaret Somerville is, in her way, all of the above, but I am referring also, of course, to Drs. Buckingham, Nathanson, and Reid, and Professor Young.) As one might expect, they do not agree on everything – the place of religion in this debate, for example,[3] or the nature of homosexuality – but they do agree that the experiment in question threatens to cut some of the main threads from which our social fabric is woven.

My own essay, and Professor DeCoste's sophisticated and compelling (I am tempted to say damning) contribution, provide opportunities to question the second form. The notion that the redefinition of marriage mandated by the courts is soundly based on equality-rights arguments and on the *Charter* suffers here a frontal assault that, if sustainable, must eradicate the comforting thought that what Canada is doing in divorcing traditional marriage is something done in the spirit of the heroic piety of Dr. King and his comrades.

That, of course, is a notion already challenged by many among those comrades, or among their descendants and beneficiaries.[4] Their voices must no doubt count for more than ours, when they ask us to reconsider our too-facile analogies between black rights and gay rights, especially on the marriage issue. Nevertheless, we may have something to say in our own voices, too. And when it has been said, it becomes possible to consider an alternative path to the one we are currently on. Ted Morton weighs in on how the *Charter*'s notwithstanding clause can and should be used as a check against judicial activism, so as to open such a path. It is the burden of the final essay, "Facing Reality," and of the Conclusion to begin pointing the way. These we urge our readers, on whose patience we rely, to read last and not first.

The third form of romanticism is challenged implicitly by all of the essays. If anything emerges with complete clarity from this little book – by dint of necessity also hasty; hence making no pretence of being comprehensive in scope or exhaustive in depth or consistent in terminology – it is that bowing for too long at the feet of our favourite symbol of civic virtue is a sure way to addle our brains. The question of the definition of marriage is not one that can be settled responsibly simply by devotion to Our Lady of Tolerance. Still, out of due respect for that marvellous lady, we offer these challenges under her protection.

Notes

1 From "Love and Marriage" by Sammy Cahn, in *Our Town*, ©1955 Barton Music Corp., renewed and assigned to Barton Music Corp. & Cahn Music Company, Los Angeles, CA.

2 Engels, to whom I will return in the final essay of this collection, argues in the tradition of modern genealogists that marriage is a highly malleable institution, and that "full freedom of marriage" can only be established when "there is no other motive left except mutual inclination." This idyllic situation can only arise, of course, with the abolition of capitalism and of the state itself; see *Origins of the Family, Private Property and the State*, chap. 2, pt. 4 (*Collected Works of Marx and Engels*, vol. 26; New York: International Publishers, 1990). For a later analysis, more immediately germane to same-sex marriage, which Engels did not have in view, see Michel Foucault's three-volume *The History of Sexuality*.

3 On the broader issue of religion in the public sphere, see Douglas Farrow, ed., *Recognizing Religion in a Secular Society* (Montreal: McGill-Queen's University Press, 2004).

4 As I write, I notice in the *Wall Street Journal* ("Marriage of Inconvenience," 23 Feb. 2004) that Jesse Jackson has added his voice to the chorus.

ONE

The Conflict

WAR OF THE RING
War of the Ring

Daniel Cere

During the 1970s and 80s, most gay and lesbian theorists rejected marriage as an incurably heterosexist institution irrelevant to their concerns. Not surprisingly, the marriage question sparked little interest in a movement that defined itself as being free at last from the constraints of heterosexual conjugality. However, by the late 1990s, marriage was becoming the focus of gay and lesbian advocacy.[1] Within a few short years, a project to impose a new public meaning on the age-old institution was being advanced. Courts and governments began to take up the cause. The gradual deregulation of marriage passed over into an effort to reconstitute marriage on a new model. The war of the ring began, and the situation in the country changed dramatically.

How did the change come about? As recently as 1999, the Parliament of Canada confidently reaffirmed the historic definition of marriage, by a vote of 216 to 55. In 2001, the first same-sex marriage case reached a Canadian provincial court, but the British Columbia Supreme Court rejected the petition, arguing that the common-law definition of marriage could not be changed without an amendment to the country's Constitution. Then, within a year, legal advocates began their full-court press. In July 2002, in *Halpern* v. *Canada*, the Ontario Superior Court challenged the existing definition of marriage. This controversial judgment was followed by two copycat decisions in the Québec Superior Court and the British Columbia Court of Appeal.[2]

The Ontario decision did not insist that marriage *must* be redefined. However, it did conclude that the existing legal framework was discriminatory since it failed to provide fair public recognition of gay and lesbian unions. *Halpern* suggested three possible remedies:[3] (a) redefine marriage as a union of two persons, or (b) establish a domestic partnership regime that would offer legal recognition for same-sex couples, or (c) abolish marriage as a category in law and set up some kind of neutral registry system. According to *Halpern*, any remedy would have to be implemented "in a manner that accords to same-sex couples a recognition that is full and equal to that enjoyed by opposite-sex couples."

The Ontario court conceded that it was setting in motion a political process that would be "contentious, divisive, troublesome, and potentially at risk of paralysis."[4] Justice Robert Blair warned that the legal redefinition of marriage would not be an incremental change but a profound one. He noted that the consequences

> flowing from such a transformation in the concept of marriage . . . are extremely complex. They will touch the core of many people's belief and value systems, and their resolution is laden with social, political, cultural, emotional and legal ramifications. They require a response to a myriad of . . . issues relating to such things as inheritance . . . , filiation, biogenetic and artificial birth technologies, adoption, and other marriage[-related] . . . matters.[5]

Halpern gave the federal government two years to consider the legislative options. If the government failed to act, the court would impose the remedy of redefining marriage.

In response to these developments, the federal government established a parliamentary committee to gauge the views of Canadians. Public hearings began in January 2003, moving across Canada from Halifax to Vancouver and travelling to Inuit communities as far north as Iqaluit. Nearly 500 submissions were made by cultural and aboriginal groups, various civil associations, and faith communities. Then another judicial bombshell. On 10 June 2003, the Ontario Court of Appeal declared that it would not bother to wait for the government, or for Canadians, to consider new legislative responses. It struck down the existing law of marriage as discriminatory, redefining marriage as a "union of two persons."

The federal government immediately hit the brakes on the parliamentary process. On 12 June, just two days after the decision, it abolished the House of Commons committee exploring this issue, sweeping aside the contributions of the numerous individuals and groups that had participated in the hearings. Less than a week later, on 17 June, the federal cabinet announced that it would draft legislation changing the definition of marriage. A few weeks after that, the government went to the Supreme Court of Canada with a set of reference questions aimed at securing its approval for the new definition. Without an electoral mandate, without the benefit of serious social-scientific research, without adequate democratic deliberation, without the normal process of judicial appeal, the government repudiated the historic definition of marriage and threw its weight behind the project to redesign that most basic of social institutions.[6]

Conjugal Marriage or Close Relationships?

Comparative cultural analysis alerts us to the great diversity of forms taken by the marital institution, but it also shows us that marriage invariably displays certain features. Summarizing the historical and cross-cultural evidence, Margo Wilson and Martin Daly, evolutionary psychologists at McMaster University, conclude that marriage is an institution that interacts with a unique social-sexual ecology in human life. It bridges the male-female divide. It negotiates a stable partnership of life and property. It seeks to manage the procreative process and to establish parental obligations to offspring. It supports the birthright of children to be connected to their mothers and fathers.[7]

Canadian law and public policy have long recognized this. In *Egan* v. *Canada*,[8] Justice La Forest summed up the legal tradition when he stated that marriage is "firmly anchored in the biological and social realities" that men and women "have the unique ability to procreate, that most children are the product of these relationships, and that they are generally cared for and nurtured by those who live in that relationship." However, by the time of *Egan*, a revolt against those realities was already well under way. A new body of academic and legal opinion was busily draining marriage of its core conjugal characteristics: permanence, pro-creativity, and child-centredness. The move to divest marriage even of its sex-bridging essence was being prepared. Conjugal marriage would be discarded in favour of something else, something built on "pure relationships" or on what scholars sometimes call "close relationship theory."[9]

> *Conjugal marriage would be discarded in favour of something else, something built on "pure relationships" or on what scholars sometimes call "close relationship theory."*

The British social theorist Anthony Giddens argues that contemporary culture is in the midst of a shift from a culture of marriage to a culture of pure relationships.[10] A pure relationship is one that has been denuded of any goal or end beyond the intrinsic emotional, psychological, or sexual satisfaction that the relationship brings to the adults involved. Pure relationships, unlike marriages, are the ever-changing product of private negotiation. In so far as marriage itself is drawn into this new culture of intimacy, it is placed on a level playing field with all other "long-term" sexual partnerships.[11] Severed from its historic roots in sex difference, permanence, and children, it becomes nothing other or more than a form of intimacy between consenting adults. It is made more pliable, open to constant renegotiation, easily contracted and easily dissolved.[12]

The close-relationship paradigm has not yet been subjected to sustained critical evaluation. Our legal establishment, however, appears very anxious to enthrone it in law. Close-relationship theory provides the framework for the recent recommendations of the Law Commission of Canada in its 2001 report *Beyond Conjugality: Recognizing and Supporting Close Personal Adult Relationships*. Its influence is also evident in recent court judgments on marriage. Consider, for example, the language of the *Halpern* appeal:

> Marriage is, without dispute, one of the most significant forms of personal relationships . . . Through the institution of marriage, individuals can publicly express their love and commitment to each other. Through this institution, society publicly recognizes expressions of love and commitment between individuals, granting them respect and legitimacy as a couple. This public

recognition and sanction of marital relationships reflect society's approbation of the personal hopes, desires and aspirations that underlie loving, committed conjugal relationships. This can only enhance an individual's sense of self-worth and dignity.[13]

What is seldom acknowledged is that this paradigm shift from the conjugal to the close relationship represents a fundamental reinterpretation of the core social purposes of marriage. We are assured that the redefinition it mandates won't make any real difference to society at large; it will simply provide a new measure of dignity to a small and oppressed minority. Evan Wolfson, a prominent same-sex marriage advocate in the United States, dismisses any concern about the big picture with a cheeky rebuke: "Gay people will not use up all the marriage licenses. There's enough marriage to share."[14]

This comforting rhetoric has a familiar ring to it, however. Thirty-five years ago advocates of the liberalization of divorce laws advanced a similar line of argument. At that time, critics of no-fault divorce cautioned that tampering with the meaning of marital permanence could affect the stability of marriage as a social institution. Opinion leaders dismissed those worries, too. No-fault divorce would only make things easier for those hard-pressed couples already headed for breakup, they insisted. Why should it affect stable marriages? There was a lot of talk about all the good things divorce reform would do for the marriage culture. Conjugal culture would be cleansed of bad marriages. Overall marital happiness would be enhanced. With this guarantee, divorce reforms were put into law. The guarantee proved to be fraudulent; divorce rates spiked dramatically, and marital satisfaction declined.[15]

Once again, the experts are confidently telling us that another radical legal change won't make much of a difference. Once again, they are telling us that making marriage more pliable and user-friendly will only enhance Canada's marriage culture. Indeed, Canadians will be able to pride themselves that the change will make their country "rather cool" when compared with other nations.[16] Such facile assurances ought to worry us. So, too, should the apparent inability, or unwillingness, to reckon forthrightly with sex-difference in our social ecology.[17] That difference is something with which close-relationship theory cannot cope. As theories go, it is a blunt instrument. Its very capacity to create "a level playing field" means that it cannot generate any insight into sexual complementarity, male-female bonding, reproduction, or the ties between parents and offspring – which makes it quite unsuitable for dealing with marriage or with marital law.[18]

A Closer Look at the Close-Relationship Experiment

A rich history and a complex heritage of symbols, myths, theologies, traditions, poetry, and art have been generated by the institution of marriage.

Michel Foucault contends that marriage has fostered a particular type of human identity, namely, the "conjugal self."[19] Be that as it may, marriage has always been the central cultural site of male-female relations. A rich history and a complex heritage of symbols, myths, theologies, traditions, poetry, and art have been generated by the institution of marriage, which encodes a unique set of aspirations into human culture along the axis of permanent opposite-sex bonding and parent-child connectedness.[20]

The proposal to delete sex-difference from the definition of marriage breaks up this code and challenges this heritage, as thoughtful gay and lesbian theorists concede. Ladelle McWhorter, for one, points out that if gay people are

> allowed to participate as gay people in the communities and institutions [heterosexuals] claim as theirs, our presence will change those institutions and practices enough to undermine their preferred version of heterosexuality and, in turn, they themselves will not be the same. [Heterosexuals] are right, for example, that if same-sex couples get legally married, the institution of marriage will change, and since marriage is one of the institutions that support heterosexuality and heterosexual identities, heterosexuality and heterosexuals will change as well.[21]

Heterosexuals are asked to overlook this fact, though it is not in their best interests to do so. Even the Ontario Court of Appeal demands, in effect, that the public meaning of marriage must be revised to take into account "the needs, capacities and circumstances of same-sex couples, not . . . the needs, capacities and circumstances of opposite-sex couples."[22] How reasonable is that, when the reconstitution of marriage to suit same-sex couples is going to have a serious impact on the community most served by the institution?

While most Canadians adhere to the historic conjugal definition of marriage, some are lulled into believing that redefinition will make little difference to their lives and families, and so into compliance with such demands.[23] But that compliance betrays a flawed understanding of the nature of social institutions. Social and economic theorists have rightly underscored the critical importance of institutions as public markers of social meaning.[24] Meaning matters, and the institutions that bear it serve to structure our experiences and to steer them in a particular direction. They define our goals, focus attention on those goals, and direct us toward them. Professor Harry Krause points out that the law "has deeply affected (and helped to affect) family behavior over time," and promises to continue to "shape and channel our future in this most important playground of human existence."[25]

We cannot tinker with the fundamentals of an institution like marriage without expecting significant consequences. Suppose the rules of chess were changed in order to standardize the moves of each of the pieces – what we would be left with would not be chess at all but a curious-looking game of checkers. Marriage, likewise, is not improved by becoming all things to all people. Rather, its capacity to carry its social meaning, and to serve its own distinctive goals, is cast into doubt. Changing the public meaning of an institution changes the social reality.[26] It transforms the understandings, practices, and goods supported by that institution. In this case it alters even the "conjugal self."[27] All of which helps to account for the highly charged nature of the conflict over marriage among those who are paying closer attention.

When we are asked for specifics about the changes that redefinition will bring, we are not altogether reduced to speculation. The couple-centred or close-relationship paradigm has been tried before. It may appear to be the latest fashion, but it has a longer and more checkered history than its advocates care to admit. In fact, today's couple-centred doctrine is a recycled version of the ideologies promulgated over the last century or so by largely discredited social theorists such as Friedrich

Engels, Margaret Mead, and Alfred Kinsey. In the 1950s, for example, Harvard's Carle Zimmermann summarized the "new" marriage doctrine being popularized by Soviet Marxists and American sexologists: Marriage must be cut loose from its traditional anchors in permanence, male-female complementarity, and procreation. Marriage must be open to the endless creation of new lifestyles and new family forms. Marriage must be about loving relationships stripped and purified of any connection to the historic commitments and purposes of marriage.[28] Sound familiar?

Already in the 1920s, the Soviet feminist Aleksandra Kollantai was an enthusiastic proponent of this vision of marriage. She believed that marriage must be liberated from the oppressive constraints of permanence and children. A new culture of marriage "would be based only on mutual love." It would rest strictly "on emotional compatibility, common interests, and erotic attraction," and "would be moral only as long as . . . love persisted."[29] Moving words, and more than a little shrewd. Kollantai had embraced Marxism and was anxious to see the "withering of marriage" from a newly emancipated society. She calculated that nudging marriage toward this more pliable notion of pure mutual love would do the trick. As Commissar of Social Welfare, Kollantai was given the opportunity to put theory into practice. The force of the Soviet state was used to implement a set of legal reforms aimed at changing the public meaning of marriage. Policies included the establishment of no-fault divorce, eliminating legal distinctions between cohabitation and marriage, reconstituting marriage as a civil-union regime, universalizing abortion, establishing universal daycare, and other reforms now familiar to Canadians as well.

By the mid-1930s, these state interventions had done some serious damage. Family life in the USSR was destabilized, divorce rates were rising, temporary cohabitation was becoming more and more prevalent, birth rates were declining, and children were falling between the cracks of broken families, often ending up in the streets. The Soviet regime finally saw the writing on the wall and attempted some restorative work; in 1936 it began reversing some of its previous legal reforms. Commissar Kollantai would be amused, however, to learn that Western societies such as Sweden, Holland, and Canada (allowing for political differences) have been treading a similar path, over the last thirty-five years, to that of pre-war Soviet society.[30] And as they slowly but surely implement many of the policies that these earlier reformers experimented with, they are documenting many of the same results: declining marriage rates, declining birth rates, rising divorce rates, more couples in ever more temporary forms of cohabitation, more people struggling as single parents, and the attendant consequences for children.[31]

As was the case in the Soviet Union, not everyone is happy with the experiment. Surveys indicate that the vast majority of young men and women still aspire to committed marriage and family life as the centrepiece of their lives. Indeed, the hunger for a good marriage seems to be more acute among young people today than it was ten years ago.[32] The indications are, however, that these aspirations will often be frustrated and defeated. Social scientists suggest that current trends will have a profound impact on the lives of the millennium generation. "What's going on now is making the sexual revolution of the '60s and '70s pale in comparison," says Dr. Eli Coleman.[33]

The vast majority of young men and women still aspire to committed marriage and family life as the centrepiece of their lives.

Surveying the scene in Canada, sociologist Zheng Wu warns that it would be foolish to underestimate either the magnitude or the tempo of the decline of marriage over the past few decades.[34] Marriage rates fell from 7.1 per thousand in 1987 to 5.1 in 1998. That makes Canada's marriage rate significantly lower than that of the United States (8.4 in 1998) or of England (10.2 in 1998). The divorce rate, which began to spike in the 1960s, now hovers around 40%. The average age for marrying has climbed steeply. In the 1960s, it was 23 for women and 26 for men; now it is 32 for women and 34 for men. (This trend is placing greater stress on women, who must contend with a less merciful biological clock.) The proportion of families headed by married couples has dropped by over 20%. Cohabitation has more than doubled since 1981. Single-parent families have risen 50% since 1981.[35]

This social drift is most pronounced in Québec, which is the trend leader in the movement toward a culture of pure relationships. Currently 30% of Québecers live in cohabitational relationships (the highest in North America). The province's marriage rates have plummeted from

8.5 in the mid-1970s to 3.0 today. Despite the low marriage rates, divorce rates remain spectacularly high, at 47%.

Canadians, in other words, are increasingly having difficulty in forming and maintaining families. They are also bringing fewer children into the world. In 2001, some 40% of married couples were childless. In 1960, the Canadian fertility rate was about 4.0. Today our birth rate has collapsed to 1.5, well below the rate of replacement (2.1); it dropped 25% in the ten years between 1992 and 2002. Québec's fertility rate is even lower at 1.4, and in that province more than half of the children born (58%) are now born outside of marriage.

During the 1970s and 1980s, the baby-boomer generation transformed marriage into a very unstable institution. However, for the vast majority, marriage remained the main hinge of male-female relationships. Things look different now. Male-female relationships no longer revolve around marriage but hang on something so indefinite as to merit only that vaguest of tags, "being in a relationship." Ironically, in the new pure-relationship culture, men and women are drawn together for shorter and shorter periods of time, leaving more and more people flying solo. The recent study by Edward Laumann et al., *The Sexual Organization of the City*,[36] points out that the majority of individuals in urban areas now spend most of their adult lives being single, interspersed with periods of temporary marriage or cohabitation. Only a minority achieve a permanent marriage; fewer and fewer conceive and raise children together.

Katherine Gilday's new National Film Board documentary, *Women and Men Unglued*, poignantly depicts the fragmentation of male-female relationships among Canada's millennium generation. As the pathways to marriage become more difficult to negotiate, many of our young adults are beginning to wonder whether stable marriage is even a possibility. And yet – it is worth repeating – young people still look to a lasting marriage and family as the key to happiness. Canadian survey research indicates that 88% of young Canadians want to marry, 88% want to stay with the same partner for life, and 92% want to have children.[37] If that is really the case, the close-relationship experiment hardly seems designed to meet their needs; nor can it rely on them for support in the long run. So whose needs *does* it serve, and why is it being deployed with such vigour?

Enforcing the New Marriage Regime

The deconstruction of conjugal marriage in Canada has not been driven by democratic demand. In fact, the ongoing legal "reform" of marriage has been imposed from the top down. There is a sociological divide on the marriage issue, with support for same-sex marriage coming disproportionately from elite sectors of society – the academy, the legal community, the upper echelons of business and government – and from the media.[38]

That is worth remembering when exposed, as one so often is, to the movement's moralizing rhetoric. Advocates of redefinition, and of the close-relationship ideology that undergirds it, are consistently presented as more caring, more compassionate, more tolerant, and more discerning than their opponents. It is regularly stated, or at least insinuated, that those who reject redefinition are motivated by prejudice, ignorance, hatred, or religious intolerance. What that says about prior generations of Canadians, or about the rest of the world for that matter, may be debated. But what it says about those Canadians – some 67%, according to survey data – who still insist on the traditional definition is only too clear. They are the great unwashed, who lack moral sense and whose voice cannot be trusted.

In the politics of persuasion, rhetoric this hot should not be above suspicion. After all, most of the same Canadians who adhere to the traditional view also applaud the overcoming of unjust discrimination; a significant number of them even want to see formal recognition of gay and lesbian unions,[39] though *not* at the cost of changing the public meaning of marriage. There is no evidence that their position is rooted in prejudice or ill will. Until recently, gays and lesbians themselves regarded marriage as an intrinsically heterosexual institution, and many still do.

Perhaps, then, it is time to stand this charge on its head. Could it be that the language of tolerance and compassion, of diversity and rights – the standard panoply of same-sex marriage rhetoric – is little more than a moralizing veneer concealing other interests? One may choose not to doubt the sincerity of the academic artisans labouring to provide creative justifications for the deconstruction project. However, as Foucault warns, self-righteous moralities often prove to be "supple mechanisms" for advancing special interests in the public market of human relationships. Sexuality and social power – indeed, economic power – are interlaced.[40]

One sign of bad faith on the part of some who wish to entrench close-relationship theory is that they rarely reveal in the political arena just how far they are prepared to go in reconceiving marriage. The opposite-sex stipulation is for them but the first of several restrictions still to be challenged in a much larger deregulation agenda. That agenda – and deregulation, not same-sex marriage per se, *is* the agenda – is already being advanced on several fronts. For example, courts have recently come to the defence of privatized prenuptial agreements that subvert the public "community of life and property" character of marriage.

> *The opposite-sex stipulation is but the first of several restrictions still to be challenged in a much larger deregulation agenda.*

In *Hartshorne* v. *Hartshorne*,[41] the Supreme Court of Canada concluded that the law must respect the fact that "individuals may choose to structure their affairs *in a number of different ways*" *and not try* "to second-guess" these freely chosen arrangements. Marriage is here nudged toward a purely private contract or barter system. The door is opened to designer marriages in which the individual partner with the greater resources calls the tune in crafting nuptial deals.

More disturbing is the fact that, off-camera, there is much talk in these circles of cracking open the dyadic restriction on marriage to make room for polygamy. Harry Krause, a respected legal theorist, notes with some satisfaction that polygamy now has "its thoroughly modern advocates."[42] Granted, but this renewed interest in polygamy should tell us something about the social-sexual interests in play here. The tradition of monogamous marriage in Western societies has always been a social practice that constrains the non-egalitarian instincts of aristocratic power. That restraining influence is now facing a serious challenge. Polygamy is the classic public-policy interest of socio-economic male elites with surplus resources to wield in the sexual marketplace.[43]

Room is to be made not only for polygamy, however, but also for polyamory. Academics now hold round-table discussions on the ethics of multiple-partner relationships. Dr. Deborah Anapol, for one, assures us that polyamory is an authentic expression of the multifaceted potential of pure-relationship culture, and so it is.[44] The opening up of marriage to multiple-partnership arrangements, when predicated on an understanding of marriage that is no longer constrained by an interest in permanent male-female bonding, procreation, and the welfare of children, is a rather obvious move. Indeed, it is difficult to see what compelling objection could be brought against it.[45]

Advocates of redefinition do not ordinarily point this out when dealing with the general public. They content themselves with the claim that a gender-neutral definition of marriage, on the close-relationship paradigm, will advance the values of fairness and tolerance. But state establishment of such a paradigm will forge for them a new ring of power, with which still more controversial transformations can be achieved. What they are asking is that law should be recast in a way that effectively denounces the conjugal conception of marriage as irrational, discriminatory, and unconstitutional, and that a new public meaning of marriage should be imposed by the sovereign power of the state. Policy decisions would then have to follow suit in all spheres of public life.[46] This winner-takes-all approach is touted as a "liberal" resolution to the debate.

If this reading of the situation seems exaggerated, consider the language that finds its way even into official court judgments. In *Halpern*, Justice LaForme declared the traditional view "repugnant."[47] *Goodridge* v. *Department of Public Health* (Massachusetts) includes passages denouncing the special privileges of marriage as a "caste-like system," support for which rests on "invidious distinctions" that are "totally repugnant."[48] Support for such distinctions is said to be "rooted in persistent prejudices against persons who are . . . homosexual." "The Constitution," we are warned, "cannot control such prejudices but neither can it tolerate them."[49]

The threats implicit in such language are not mitigated in the least by a government that promises, as the Canadian government recently did, not to coerce clergy into solemnizing unions against their beliefs. It is cold comfort to know that the state has no plans to do what is seldom even contemplated by totalitarian regimes. And is it not revealing that, in this new legal landscape, such a strange peril should appear on the horizon?

A Time to Choose

In the glow of the Liberal government's landmark decision to change the definition of marriage, one of the leading advocates of same-sex marriage, New Democrat MP Svend Robinson, was asked whether he and his partner would soon be wearing wedding rings. The *Globe and Mail* (24 June 2003) recorded his response: "It's been an incredible time for those of us who have struggled for full recognition of gay and lesbian couples' equality rights. Yet I'm still unsure if Max and I will marry anytime soon. After nine years in a committed, loving relationship, how would the state's imprimatur change anything?" Some were confused by Robinson's response. Wasn't gaining that imprimatur the whole point of the struggle to force a redefinition of marriage? Was Robinson somehow dismissing the struggle as unimportant after all? Was he making light of it? On the contrary, if we stop to think about it, we can see that his dilemma was a perfectly natural one.

Marriage, on the historic conjugal view, is a union that includes, but also transcends, the subjective interests of the couple. It shapes the way they act as a couple and the way society acts toward them. It spells out a set of responsibilities and a social protocol. Through its recognition of marriage, the state affirms and promises to support those who accept the challenge of building a permanent and exclusive bond with a person of the opposite sex, a bond that opens outwards toward the future of society through the possibility of conceiving and rearing children. Marriage, to that extent, is a public affair.[50]

On the close-relationship model, however, marriage is reduced to a formalization of one's emotional commitment to a sexual partner. How exactly this kind of marriage serves society is open to debate. Society's support for it has none the less been demanded, in the name of equality, and for this the state's imprimatur is necessary. Once that support has been granted, though – once same-sex marriage has been established as a legal testimony to the full equality of close relationships in general – it is far from obvious why any particular close relationship should be bothered with it. If marriage means little more than having the state involved in one's love relationship, then a studied indifference to it may well be the right approach.

It is sometimes observed that same-sex couples like Svend and Max constitute a minute fraction of the population – well under 1% of all married and cohabiting couples in the country[51] – and that the commitment of these couples to a marriage culture remains uncertain. So perhaps we can all afford to be a little bit indifferent. No matter what happens to the law, same-sex marriages in Canada will surely be few.

That is true enough. But what is at stake in the war of the ring cannot be measured in simple, quantitative terms. Svend's dilemma should remind us of the fact that the battle for marriage is ultimately a battle for public meaning, and that public meaning really does matter. Redefining marriage is a high-risk game for the huge sector of Canadian society sustained by this institution. As a nation guided by the rule of law, we can't have it both ways. Under the rubric of "marriage," we will either have an institution dedicated to male-female bonding, and to procreation and child-rearing, or we will have a quite different institution, dedicated to a close-relationships regime. We, too, must choose, and our choice will make a qualitative, as well as a quantitative, difference to our future.

Notes

1 Cf. David Chambers, "Couples: Marriage, Civil Union, and Domestic Partnership" in *Creating Change: Sexuality, Public Policy, and Civil Rights*, John D'Emelio, William B. Turner, Urvashi Vaid, eds. (New York: St. Martin's Press, 2002), pp. 281–304.

2 *Halpern v. Canada (A.G.)*, [2002] 60 O.R. (3d) 321 (Ont. Div. Ct.) [hereinafter *Halpern* (2002)]; *Hendricks v. Quebec (A.G.)*, [2002] J.Q. No. 3816 (Sup. Ct.); *Barbeau v. British Columbia (A.G.)*, 2003 BCCA 251.

3 *Halpern* (2002), ibid. at para. 127ff.

4 Ibid. at para. 138.

5 Ibid., at paras. 97–99: "The Courts are not the best equipped to conduct such a balancing exercise, in my opinion. This is not an incremental change in the law. It is a profound change. Although there may be historical examples of the acceptance of same-sex unions, everyone acknowledges that the institution of marriage has been commonly understood and accepted for centuries as the union of a man and a woman. Deep-seated cultural, religious, and socio-political mores have evolved and shaped society's views of family, child-rearing and protection, and 'couple-hood' based upon that heterosexual view of marriage. The apparent simplicity of a linguistic change in the wording of a law does not necessarily equate with an incremental change in that law. To say that altering the common law meaning of marriage to include same-sex unions is an incremental change, in my view, is to strip the word 'incremental' of its meaning." (Justice Robert Blair)

6 The Québec Court of Appeal, in *Ligue catholique pour les droits de l'homme* v. *Hendricks*, [2004] J.Q. No. 2593 (Qc. C.A.), underlined the legal significance of the federal government's failure to contest recent court decisions declaring the traditional definition constitutionally invalid (para. 24). A federal law cannot be unacceptable in one province yet acceptable in others. If the traditional definition of marriage is unacceptable in Ontario, then it is unacceptable in all of Canada (para. 28). The court thus concluded that recent judicial and political manoeuvres have effectively killed the historic definition of marriage in Canada.

7 "Marriage is a universal social institution, albeit with myriad variations in social and cultural details. A review of the cross-cultural diversity in marital arrangements reveals certain common themes: some degree of mutual obligation between husband and wife, a right of sexual access (often but not necessarily exclusive), an expectation that the relationship will persist (although not necessarily for a lifetime), some cooperative investment in offspring, and some sort of recognition of the status of the couple's children. The marital alliance is fundamentally a reproductive alliance . . . " Margo Wilson and Martin Daly, "Marital Cooperation and Conflict" in *Evolutionary Psychology, Public Policy and Personal Decision*, Charles Crawford and Catherine Salmon, eds. (Mahwah, NJ: Lawrence Erlbaum Associates, 2004), p. 203.

8 [1995] 2 S.C.R. 513 [hereinafter *Egan*].

9 "Close-relationship theory" focuses on the common dynamics – initiation, maintenance, dissolution – present in *all* sexually bonded relationships. The case for same-sex marriage is based on the close-relationship assumption thst same-sex relationships are equivalent. In *The Case for Same-Sex Marriage* (New York: Free Press, 1996), p. 109, fn. 6, William Eskridge, Jr., leans on Letitia Anne Peplau and Susan D. Cochrane's "A Relationship Perspective on Homosexuality," in David P. McWhirter et al., *Homosexuality/Heterosexuality: Concepts of Sexual Orientation* (New York: Oxford University Press, 1990).

10 See Anthony Giddens, *The Transformation of Intimacy: Sexuality, Love and Eroticism in Modern Societies* (Cambridge: Polity Press, 1994), and *Modernity and Self-identity. Self and Society in the Late Modern Age* (Cambridge: Polity Press, 1992).

11 Close-relationship theory bleaches out the significance of embodied sexual difference and argues that all committed sexual bonds should be "subsumed under the broader construct of close or *primary* relationships." John Scanzoni et al., *The Sexual Bond: Rethinking Families and Close Relationships* (Newbury Park, CA: Sage Publications, 1989), p. 9. For a critique of close-relationship theory, see Daniel Cere, "Courtship Today: The View from Academia" in *Public Interest* 143 (Spring 2001): 53–71.

12 David R. Shumway, *Modern Love: Romance, Intimacy and the Marriage Crisis* (New York: New York University Press, 2003), pp. 139–40; Don Edgar, "Globalization and Western Bias in Family Sociology" in Jacqueline Scott, Judith Treas, and Martin Richards, eds., *The Blackwell Companion to the Sociology of Families* (Oxford: Blackwell, 2004), pp. 3–16.

13 *Halpern* v. *Canada* (2003), O.A.C. 172 at para. 5 [hereinafter *Halpern*].

14 Ben Townley, "U.S. Gay Marriage Debate Rumbles On" (www.uk.gay.com 20 Oct. 2003).

15 See the discussion of Canadian developments by Douglas W. Allen, "Comments on the Justice Minister's Same-Sex Discussion Paper," 1 Apr. 2003 (www.marriageinstitute.ca).

16 "Canada's New Spirit," *The Economist*, 25 Sept. 2003.

17 Advocates of redefinition do occasionally recognize these substantive differences. Cf. William Eskridge, Jr., *Gaylaw: Challenging Apartheid in the Closet* (Cambridge, MA: Harvard University Press, 1999), p. 11.

18 The close-relationship model discovers exactly what it predicts, namely, that same-sex relationships share certain common features with opposite-sex relationships. Thus Justice Blair (*Halpern*, supra note 13 at para. 32) went so far as to say that the former may be "marriage-like in everything but name." But it must be pointed out that close-relationship theory searches for common interpersonal dynamics in all intimate relationships. These patterns hold true for all dyadic relationships – friendship, sibling, same-sex, and opposite-sex relationships. Cf. Susan S. Hendrick, *Understanding Close Relationships* (Boston: Pearson Educational, 2003), pp. 108–9.

19 Michel Foucault, *The History of Sexuality*, vol. 3 (New York: Vintage, 1988), pp. 72–80.

20 Suzanne Frayser, *Varieties of Sexual Experience* (New Haven, CT: HRAF Press, 1985) and George Murdock, *Social Structure* (New York: Free Press, 1965).

21 Ladelle McWhorter, *Bodies and Pleasures: Foucault and the Politics of Sexual Normalization* (Bloomington: Indiana University Press, 1999), p. 125.

22 This on the basis that "the purpose and effects of the impugned law must at all times be viewed from the perspective of the claimant" (*Halpern*, supra note 13 at para. 91).

23 See Dimitra Pantazopoulos, *Ethix: Where Canadians Stand on the Ethical, Moral and Value Issues of the Day*, COMPAS Public Opinion Poll Analysis, Praxis Public Strategies, 28 Nov. 2003.

24 On the "new institutionalism" see, e.g., James M. Acheson, ed., *Anthropology and Institutional Economics* (New York: University of America Press, 1994). For its impact on the study of human sexuality, see Stephen Ellington, Edward O. Laumann, Anthony Paik, and Jenna Mahay, "The Theory of Sex Markets" in *The Sexual Organization of the City*, Edward Laumann et al., eds. (Chicago: University of Chicago Press, 2004), pp. 24–30.

25 Harry Krause, "Marriage for the New Millennium: Heterosexual, Same-Sex – or Not At All?" in *Family Law Quarterly* 34 (2000): 284–85.

26 Wolfgang Kasper and Manfred Streit describe institutions as "the 'software' that channels the interaction of people." In *Institutional Economics: Social Order and Public Policy* (Cheltenham, UK: Edward Elgar, 1998), p. 6. See also Edward Schiappa, *Defining Reality: Definitions and the Politics of Meaning* (Carbondale and Edwardsville: Southern Illinois University Press, 2003) and *On the Nature of Social and Institutional Reality*, E. Lagerspetz, H. Ihaheimo, and J. Kotkavirta, eds. (Sophi: University of Juvaskyla, 2001).

27 Alasdair MacIntyre and others have argued that social institutions are "practices" that embody certain internal goods as well as producing certain external goods.

See *After Virtue* (South Bend, IN: University of Notre Dame Press, 1981). The self is shaped by its orientation to these goods. Institutions thus provide unique contexts for pursuing and actualizing particular forms of self-identity, which, as Mary Douglas says, are deeply connected to "defining communities"; see *How Institutions Think* (Syracuse, NY: Syracuse University Press, 1986), chap. 9.

28 See Zimmerman's *Family and Civilization* (New York: Harper and Brothers, 1947), chap. 2.

29 Quoted in Lynn D. Wardle, "The 'Withering Away' of Marriage: Some Lessons from the Bolshevik Family Law Reforms in Russia, 1917–1926" (II, B. 1, 2). For more on the present subject, see H. Kent Geiger, *The Family in Soviet Russia* (Cambridge, MA: Harvard University Press, 1968) and Harold J. Berman, "Soviet Family Law in Light of Russian History and Marxist Theory" in *Yale Law Journal* 26 (1946).

30 See, e.g., Allan Carlson's *The Swedish Experiment in Family Politics* (New Brunswick, NJ: Transaction, 1990) and Brigitte Berger's *The Family in the Modern Age* (New Brunswick, NJ: Transaction, 2002), chap. 2.

31 Research indicates that the reduction of marriage to a pliable close-personal-relationship regime means more unstable and less child-centred marriages. See Maggie Gallagher and Linda Waite, *The Case for Marriage* (New York: Doubleday, 2000), chap. 2; David R. Hall, "Risk Society and the Second Demographic Transition" in *Canadian Studies in Population* 29 (2002): 173–93; Frank Cox, "Qualities of Strong and Resilient Families" in *Human Intimacy: Marriage, the Family and Its Meaning* (Belmont, CA: Wadsworth Publishing, 1999), pp. 4–6.

32 The proportion of Americans between the ages of 18 and 29 who told interviewers that a "happy marriage" is an important part of the "good life" actually increased between 1991 and 1996, from 72% to 86%. See Ira Mark Gellman, "Divorce Rates, Marriage Rates, and the Problematic Persistence of Traditional Marital Roles" in *Family Law Quarterly* 34.1 (Spring 2000): 17.

33 Quoted from Martha Irvine, "Survey Reveals Real-Life Sex and the City," CNN.COM, 9 Jan. 2004, http://www.cnn.com/2004/US/01/09/urban.coupling.ap/; cf. David Hall's talk of a "second demographic transition."

34 "Recent Trends in Marriage Patterns in Canada" in *Policy Options*, Sept. 1998. For summaries of Canadian statistical data see "Updates on Families" in *Canadian Social Trends* 69 (2003); John Conway, *The Canadian Family in Crisis* (Toronto: James Lorimer, 2003); Joanne Paetsch, Nicholas Bala, Lorne Bertrand, and Lisa Glennon, "Trends in the Formation and Dissolution of Couples" in *The Blackwell Companion to the Sociology of Families*, Jacqueline Scott, Judith Treas, and Martin Richards, eds. (Oxford: Blackwell, 2004), pp. 306–31. For American trends, see William Axinn and Arland Thornton, "The Transformation of the Meaning of Marriage" in *The Ties that Bind: Perspectives on Marriage and Cohabitation*, Linda Waite et al., eds. (New York: Aldine de Gruyter, 2000), pp. 147–65; also J. DaVanzo and M.O. Rahman, "American Families: Trends and Correlates" in *Population Index* 59 (1993): 350–86.

35 Data taken from *Statistics Canada* and *Institut de la Statistique Québec*.

36 See n. 24 above.

37 Reginald Bibby, *Canada's Teens: Today, Yesterday, and Tomorrow* (Toronto: Stoddart Publishing, 2001), pp. 143–46. In America, 93% rate marriage as one of their most important life goals (Gallagher and Waite, *The Case for Marriage*, p. 23). Brigitte Berger (*The Family in the Modern Age*, p. 59) states that "the vast majority of American men and women have remained loyal to the ideals of the conventional family . . . According to a 1996 census report most American families are still headed up by married couples (78 percent to be precise), marital bonds are still seen as binding (98 percent think marital infidelity to be wrong according to a 1996 University of Chicago sex survey), and . . . most Americans are passionately committed to their children and claim to be guided by conventional principles in the socialization of their children."

38 Canadians unencumbered by marriage, as well as those who have been involved in cohabitational relationships, also indicate more support for this couple-centred view. But it remains the case that proponents of a pure-relationship culture are distinguished by a specific social character (cf. Peter Berger, "General Observations on Normative Conflicts and Mediation" in Peter Berger, ed., *The Limits of Social Cohesion* [Boulder, CO: Westview Press, 1998]). It is also worth noting that lower-income sectors of society are more negatively affected than elite sectors by "decline of marriage" trends. See Theodore Ooms, "Strengthening Couples and Marriage in Low-Income Communities" in *Revitalizing the Institution of Marriage for the Twenty-first Century*, Alan Hawkins, Lynn Wardle, and David Orgon Coolidge, eds. (Westport, CT: Praeger, 2002), chap. 7.

39 Some 37% (i.e., more than half of those who support the traditional definition); see again Pantazopoulos, *Ethix*.

40 Cf. Michel Foucault's analysis of the modern movement toward sexual liberalization in *The History of Sexuality*, vol. 1 (New York: Vintage Books, 1990).

41 2004 SCC 22.

42 "Marriage for the New Millennium," p. 289. I want to underscore here that what drives all of these developments is a relentless push for the deregulation of marriage by reducing it to a close-relationship regime. Deleting sex-difference as a defining rule does not by itself necessitate these other developments. It is just one move in a larger political game that reaches back to earlier "reforms" and forward to still more controversial transformations.

43 Laura L. Betzig, *Despotism and Differential Reproduction* (Hawthorne, NY: Aldine De Gruyter, 1986).

44 Deborah Anapol, *Polyamory, the New Love Without Limits: Secrets of Sustainable Intimate Relationships* (San Raphael, CA: Intinet Resource Center, 1997). Roger Rubin, former vice-president of the National Council on Family Relationships, argues that the current movement to redefine marriage "has set the stage for a broader discussion over which relationships should be legally recognized." The principles used in support of same-sex marriage are also appealed to in support of polyamorous relationships. See Rubin's "Alternative Lifestyles Today" in M. Coleman and L.H. Ganong, eds., *Handbook of Contemporary Families* (Thousand Oaks, CA: Sage Publications, 2004), pp. 32–33.

45 The Law Commission has already proposed that their new legal category of "close personal relationship" should not be "limited to two people." They

argue that "the values and principles of autonomy and state neutrality require that people be free to choose the form and nature of their close personal adult relationships." *Beyond Conjugality*, p. 133, fn. 16.

46 Cf. Jack Knight and Jean Ensminger, "Conflict Over Changing Social Norms: Bargaining, Ideology, and Enforcement" in Mary Brinton and Victor Nee, eds., *The New Institutionalism in Sociology* (New York: Russell Sage Foundation, 1998), pp. 105–26.

47 *Halpern* (2002), supra note 2 at para. 411. His use of the term "repugnant" is a technical one, but cf. para. 212.

48 No. 08860 (Mass. S.J.C. 2003). On 18 Nov. 2003 the court rendered an American version of *Halpern*, with a four-three decision in favour of same-sex marriage. The quoted phrases are drawn from the opinion of Justice Greaney; see also "Opinion to the Senate," 3 Feb. 2004 (section 3 of the opinion of Justices Marshall, Greaney, Ireland, and Cowin).

49 Chief Justice Marshall (section. 3), who in the final sentence above is quoting, in a new context, a statement from *Palmore* v. *Sidoti*, 466 U.S. 429, 433 (1984).

50 See Gallagher and Waite, *The Case for Marriage*, chap. 2.

51 Recent census data in other Western countries indicate a range of about one-half to one percent.

CONFUSION ON THE HILL
Confusion on the Hill

John McKay

The view from the Hill is not a clear one at all. Canadians are deeply ambivalent about same-sex marriage, and that ambivalence is reflected both in the polls and in their choice of whom to send to Parliament. Many Members of Parliament, including some political leaders, fervently wish the issue would just go away. But it won't. Parliamentarians and citizens, like the courts, have decisions to take. My purpose here is to provide a brief backgrounder for those who are still trying to get a handle on the political and legal situation.

Let's back up a little and begin with the Fathers of Confederation, who were not nearly as confused or disturbed about the subject as we are. The historic definition of marriage as "the voluntary union for life of one man and one woman, to the exclusion of all others," contained in *Hyde* v. *Hyde and Woodmansee*, was thought to be self-evident, at least "in Christendom."[1] None of our nation's founders supposed that this definition needed to be included in the Constitution. When the Fathers of Confederation assigned marriage and divorce to the federal government, no one even considered the possibility that the definition of marriage would be challenged and reviewed.

Over the next century or so, their assumptions held. Those wanting to challenge the laws of consanguinity or numerical restriction, for example, were met with a judicial sensibility reflecting much the same values and mores, and with a stable legal tradition. By the 1980s, however, important developments had begun to take place.

Enter, the *Charter*

In 1981, Canadian politicians decided to shake up the constitutional order by passing the *Canadian Charter of Rights and Freedoms*. It was hailed then as a landmark document, and it is still embraced with enthusiasm by the vast majority of Canadians. Indeed, many see the *Charter* as fundamental to the way we define ourselves as a nation. It gives tangible expression to our growing interest in and valuation of human rights. As Michael Ignatieff explains in his book *The Rights Revolution*, "rights talk" has become increasingly irresistible to us, especially as we respond to violations of human rights beyond our borders. "I have learned," he says, "that human beings value some things more than their own survival, and that rights are the language in which they commonly express the values they are willing to die for."[2]

   Others, however, view the *Charter* in a much different light, criticizing the document for what they predicted it would do – shift an enormous amount of power over to the judicial branch of government. One of the most vocal naysayers at the time was Premier Sterling Lyon, then the premier of Manitoba and now a Justice of the Queen's Bench. Premier Lyon was prominent among those who saw the *Charter* as a move to reallocate authority from those who attain their position through election to those who attain their position through appointment. He worried that the power to define law and determine rights was being given to those who were immune to review or censure by the people. Since then, some have begun to describe judges as the new magisterium.

> *T*he power to define law and determine rights was being given to those who were immune to review or censure by the people.

   At all events, judges now had in their hands a new tool to redress wrongs, both real and perceived. New doctrines were created that allowed the judiciary to enlarge the scope of the *Charter* to suit the occasion. Legal scholars saw the Constitution as a "living tree" that was "ever greening," to allow for whatever the desired end product happened to be. Judges are certainly not infallible, however, and the *Charter*, since its introduction, has sparked an animated debate over judicial encroachment on legislative authority.

One of the most vigorous assaults on the authority of Parliament has been the use of the concept of "analogous grounds." From its inception, the *Charter* prohibited discrimination against identifiable categories such as race, sex, religion, and ethnicity. Some courts, however, felt that these categories were not exhaustive, and so proceeded to use analogous grounds to "read in" to the *Charter* things they thought belonged there, even if Parliament had left them out.

"Sexual orientation" was quickly read in, and a whole new body of law was developed whereby government could not discriminate against people based on their sexual orientation. These laws were written largely to target discrimination in the areas of employment, the receipt of pensions, and in relation to medical treatment and access to services. With this branch of the ever-greening tree secured, the area of spousal rights was then created, which saw a variety of amendments to provincial bills and the enactment of Bill C-23, *An Act to modernize the Statutes of Canada in relation to benefits and obligations*.[3] The preamble to the latter, it should be noted, specifically states that nothing in the bill alters or affects the definition of marriage.

Meanwhile, legal cases that would underpin the main assault on "marriage" were making their way through various lower courts. But worries about a coming legal storm seemed alarmist. The Supreme Court of Canada, in 1995, opined regarding *Nesbit and Egan* that nothing in the judgment being handed down would affect the definition of marriage as the union of one man and one woman to the exclusion of all others. As the court said:

Marriage has from time immemorial been firmly grounded in our legal tradition, one that is itself a reflection of long-standing philosophical and religious traditions. But its ultimate *raison d'être* transcends all of these and is firmly anchored in the biological and social realities that heterosexual couples have the unique ability to procreate, that most children are the product of these relationships, and that they are generally cared for and nurtured by those who live in that relationship. In this sense, marriage is by nature heterosexual. It would be possible to legally define marriage to include homosexual couples, but this would not change the biological and social realities that underlie the traditional marriage.[4]

We can see now, however, that those who were ringing the alarm bells were not being paranoid. The central objective of "gay marriage" advocates is to see a forced acceptance of their particular view of marriage established into law. They are no longer interested in, or satisfied with, a mere absence of discrimination against those who practise homosexual lifestyles. Rather, they are interested in moving society beyond tolerance to legally entrenched acceptance, if not approval. As the *Globe and Mail* commented in January 2004, "The first stage of any fight for equality is the quest for tolerance. The second is the quest for acceptance." At this point, said the *Globe*, "gays and lesbians in Canada are well on their way to passing through the first stage."[5]

Going With the Flow

One premise of the argument for redefining marriage, whether that argument takes place inside or outside the courtroom, is that marriage is a "love" institution – nothing more and nothing less. It should not matter, therefore, just how you are having your sex. To limit marriage by insisting that it is heterosexual in nature is simply discriminatory and cannot be tolerated in a free and democratic society.

That line of argument, as others have pointed out, is question-begging. Is marriage *really* just a love institution, or is there more to marriage than that? No less an authority than the Ontario Court of Appeal in *Halpern* v. *Canada (A.G.)*[6] takes the dumbed-down view of marriage. It dismisses as nice, but not necessary, all those other elements of cultural significance that men and women have normally taken into consideration when deciding to join each other in marriage. All that stuff about procreation, or about married couples bridging the genera-

All that stuff about procreation, or about married couples bridging the generations and ensuring the continuation of society, is dispensable if you accept the view that marriage is just a love institution.

tions and ensuring the continuation of society, is dispensable if you accept the view that marriage is just a love institution. In a modern society, according to this court, marriage is simply about the intimacy between two people; the rest is merely anachronism.

Courts such as the *Halpern* court, in other words, have taken it on themselves to reduce the institution of marriage to a warm and fuzzy sentimental core. This actually fits quite nicely with a rather colder legal tendency, in which the rich conception of marriage as a broad-based social covenant gives way to the much poorer conception of contract law. The contractual view of marriage may give comfort to lawyers, but it further erodes the mystique of marriage and undermines the foundational role that the institution plays. For marriage in the Western (Judeo-Christian) tradition is much more than a contract. It is a covenant, a social estate, a spiritual association, and a participation in God's own blessing of humanity through the promise of a human future. As an increasingly secular state, however, Canada has embraced the contractual conception and diminished all other aspects of marriage, without bothering to count the cost of this diminishment. One cost is that marriage suddenly appears discriminatory, and the country becomes divided over it.

Just how divided quickly became evident to those of us who sat on the House of Commons Justice Committee which, beginning in November 2002, worked its way across the country, hearing hundreds of witnesses on the subject of same-sex marriage. We heard much about marriage as a love institution, and much about the pain of discrimination. Similarly, we heard much about marriage as something more than a love institution, and about the pain caused by charges of discrimination. In these hearings, attempts were sometimes made at counting the costs, and the committee experienced internally as well as externally the conflicts created by the different models of marriage in play. However, before the committee could reach its conclusions or submit its report, the Ontario Court of Appeal spoke, deciding the issue for us by taking one side in the debate. It threw its *Charter* trump card on the table and brought democratic play to a halt.

When the *Halpern* decision came down on 10 June 2003, granting marriage to same-sex couples, the Justice Committee had its first (and, as it turned out, its only) draft in hand. But neither this fact, nor the

1999 House of Commons resolution in support of the common-law definition, nor yet the legislative affirmation of that definition in Bill C-23, could stop the judicial juggernaut. The federal government, which had been content to watch quietly from the sidelines, decided now to go with the flow. The justice minister, Martin Cauchon, announced that there would be no appeal. Instead, the government would put three questions to the Supreme Court of Canada on a reference, attaching a draft bill to implement same-sex marriage. The questions referred to the Supreme Court were these:

1. Is the annexed *Proposal for an Act respecting certain aspects of legal capacity for marriage for civil purposes* within the exclusive legislative authority of the Parliament of Canada? If not, in what particular or particulars, and to what extent?
2. If the answer to question 1 is yes, is section 1 of the proposal, which extends capacity to marry to persons of the same sex, consistent with the *Canadian Charter of Rights and Freedoms*? If not, in what particular or particulars, and to what extent?
3. Does the freedom of religion guaranteed by paragraph 2(a) of the *Canadian Charter of Rights and Freedoms* protect religious officials from being compelled to perform a marriage between two persons of the same sex that is contrary to their religious beliefs?

On 29 January 2004, after Paul Martin had replaced Jean Chrétien as prime minister, the new justice minister, Irwin Cotler, added a fourth question:

4. Is the opposite-sex requirement for marriage for civil purposes, as established by the common law and set out for Québec in s. 5 of the *Federal Law-Civil Law Harmonization Act, No. 1*, consistent with the *Canadian Charter of Rights and Freedoms*? If not, in what particular or particulars, and to what extent?

But the justice minister also declared the government's intention to seek a negative response to this question. Moreover, the Supreme Court still was not asked its opinion on the efficacy of a solution based on civil unions. The Justice Committee had been told that civil unions were beyond the constitutional authority of the government of Canada. Many witnesses and members, however, thought that the civil-union option for same-sex couples should have been explored.

All of this did relatively little to resolve the confusion on the Hill. Even some government members felt betrayed by the sudden decision to adopt the *Halpern* way of thinking. As one colleague put it in a *Globe and Mail* opinion piece:

> The Ontario Court of Appeal's decision to uphold same-sex partnerships last June was like a grenade dropped into the Liberal caucus. Many caucus members have expressed views on both process and content that differ from the government's response to the ruling. No one should be surprised at the apparent division in the caucus . . . Many MPs, reflecting the commonly held view of the vast majority of their constituents, maintain that marriage cannot be treated like any other invention or program of government. Marriage serves as the basis for social organization; it is not a consequence of it. Marriage signifies a particular relationship among the many unions that individuals freely enter; it's the one between a man and a woman that has two obvious goals: mutual support and procreation . . . The Ontario court offers a different description of marriage: an institution through which society publicly recognizes expressions of love and commitment between individuals.[7]

The flow, in other words, is not all in the same direction, as the most recent Commons vote on the definition of marriage showed.[8]

Parliament and Pluralism

The genius of parliamentary democracy is to create a legislative space in which a wide array of deeply held views can be considered, and laws fashioned that command general assent. Parliament – much more than the courts, which are restricted by the binary nature of their own decision-making process – is capable of working on the principle that mutual compromise and accommodation can also respect rights. Undue deference to judicial decision-making limits Parliament's proper latitude here, and that is what we have seen thus far. Put more provocatively, Parliament is in danger of becoming a mere irrelevancy in the same-sex marriage debate.

That is something that must change, and change quickly. "The role of government in our pluralist society," argues Gerald Vandezande, "is to do public justice for all, and to devise public policies that meet the basic needs and respect the fundamental rights and freedoms of all Canadians, without discrimination, including respect for other people's religious values." Making direct reference to the current debate, he adds: "It's important that in the final drafting of legislation on marriage, we do public justice to the mosaic that constitutes Canada and the diversity of human relationships.[9]

Looked at in this light, the reference questions sent to the Supreme Court are inadequate. The absence of a civil-unions option is one inadequacy, for that option speaks to the possibility of compromise and accommodation. But another inadequacy is glaringly evident in the third reference question, which invites the court's opinion on the protection of religious officials who refuse to marry same-sex couples. Having adopted the faulty premise that couple-centric marriage is the *only* legitimate view, the government here signals its intention not to prosecute those who, for religious reasons, persist in the error that marriage is much more than a love institution and is by nature heterosexual. Yet there is a high probability that religious officials who act on this "erroneous" view will be exposed to prosecution. Some of them fear, quite understandably, that they are next in the line of attack. One means of attack may be for same-sex couples to ask religious institutions for the use of their facilities for a same-sex ceremony or reception and, when refused, to sue on the grounds of discrimination.

Already we have seen civic officials in British Columbia being told that they must perform same-sex ceremonies or risk their employment.[10] With respect to religious ceremonies, it will be said that those who refuse to marry same-sex couples commit a prohibited act of discrimination, but that they are "saved" by a narrow exception clause. One can only wonder, however, how long that exception will be allowed to stand, and what other pressures will be brought to bear in the meantime through the review of tax exemptions, education permits, broadcast licences, etc. After all, how can a society continue to offer exemptions and privileges to institutions, such as churches and religious schools, that routinely "discriminate" against same-sex couples wishing to marry?

Representatives of religious communities have expressed their deep apprehension concerning equality before the law, when officials from various human-rights commissions have stated unequivocally that such behaviour is discriminatory. Little wonder that they do not expect fair treatment when other issues arise. Even some members of the Justice Committee were extraordinarily skeptical of the reassurances being offered by the government.

The threat to genuine pluralism represented by the *Halpern* decision, and by the compliant response of the executive branch, is something that the Canadian public has been watching with increasing apprehension. At the beginning of the Justice Committee hearings in November 2002, we were told that Canadians slightly favoured "gay marriage." As the debate unfolded, however, that support began to dip. And now, as pollsters have begun to ask meaningful questions, support has taken a definite downward trajectory – something of a miracle, given the obvious determination of the media's talking heads to keep bolstering that support.

Irshad Manji, an outspoken Canadian activist and gay-friendly Islamic reformer, points out that our maturity as citizens relates directly to our willingness to defend "the very pluralism of interpretations and values that makes it possible for us to be here in the first place."[11] Something similar might be said of Parliament. The confusion on the Hill cannot be settled by the Supreme Court, even if that court wisely undertakes to reinforce Parliament's sense of its own jurisdictional and legislative competence. It will be settled only when Parliament works together with the citizenry it represents to find

> *The confusion on the Hill cannot be settled by the Supreme Court, even if that court wisely undertakes to reinforce Parliament's sense of its own jurisdictional and legislative competence.*

a solution to the same-sex marriage debate that truly accommodates profound differences of opinion, while determining what best makes for the common good.

Notes

1 "I conceive," wrote Lord Penzance (1866 L.R. 1 P. & D. 130, at p. 133), "that marriage, as understood in Christendom, may for this purpose be defined as the voluntary union for life of one man and one woman, to the exclusion of all others." Since then marriage has come to be defined in common law as "the lawful and voluntary union of one man and one woman to the exclusion of all others."

2 Michael Ignatieff, *The Rights Revolution* (Toronto: Anansi, 2000), p. 3.

3 2nd Session, 36th Parliament, assented to 29 June 2000.

4 *Egan* v. *Canada*, [1995] 2 S.C.R. 513 at 515.

5 "A Marker of Gay Equality," *Globe and Mail* (2 Jan. 2004), p. A14.

6 [2002] 60 O.R. (3d) 321 (Ont. Div. Ct.)

7 Joe Volpe, "Same-Sex Marriage," *Globe and Mail* (12 Aug. 2003, online).

8 The debate on Stephen Harper's motion (16 Sept. 2003; see *Hansard* 120, beginning at 1010) and the subsequent vote – which was far from being a free vote or one uncomplicated by party manoeuvring – demonstrated the continuing substantial support in the House for traditional marriage.

9 Gerald Vandezande, "Martin's Idea of Justice," *National Post*, 30 Jan. 2004, p. A5.

10 Vital Statistics Agency CEO Andrew McBride is quoted as writing in a letter to the province's marriage commissioners, "It is necessary that I ask those marriage commissioners who feel they cannot solemnize same-sex marriages, to resign their appointments effective March 31, 2004" (Mike Choinard, "A Question of Morals and the Law," *Chilliwack Times*, 17 Feb. 2004, p. 1).

11 "A Muslim Plea for Introspection," *Globe and Mail*, 8 Nov. 2001, available online on Ms. Manji's homepage.

TWO

The Casualties

THE FUTURE OF AN EXPERIMENT

The Future of an Experiment

Katherine K. Young and Paul Nathanson

Our collaboration is based on the conviction that current debates over marriage must be assessed not only in connection with historical and cross-cultural research into the function and meaning of marriage but also in connection with the risks involved in redefining marriage. To help correct biases, our approach involves dialogue. One of us is a man, the other a woman. One is a Jew, the other a gentile. One specializes in Western civilization, the other in Eastern civilizations. And one is gay, the other straight. Neither of us opposes gay relationships or civil unions for gay people.

Given the importance of marriage in every society, the burden of proof – morally and to some extent legally[1] – surely lies with those who want to make dramatic changes. In other words, it is their responsibility to show that these changes are likely to improve society or, at the very least, unlikely to damage it. So far, advocates of gay marriage have not done so. They have merely declared either that "things will stay the same" or that "things are always changing." As if people were completely at the mercy of random historical forces (ones that just happen, however, to serve the interests of a particular group). They want to indulge in a massive experiment, albeit one that began decades ago, leaving future generations to pick up the pieces.

In this paper, we examine the following: (1) prevalent assumptions about marriage; (2) the defining features of marriage; (3) the alleged precedents for gay marriage; and (4) the possible effects of gay marriage.

Prevalent Assumptions About Marriage

We begin by challenging four underlying assumptions. Being underlying assumptions, of course, these are always unstated. Even so, the arguments based on them are quickly becoming conventional wisdom in the most influential academic and political circles. Opposing them, therefore, will necessarily involve counterintuitive and "politically incorrect" arguments. The assumptions are as follows: (a) extreme individualism; (b) emotionalism; (c) social constructionism; and (d) the idea that society is infinitely flexible. Gay people did not invent these assumptions, by the way; straight people did.

Extreme individualism: Many people, including those who demand gay marriage, now assume that the rights of individuals (or, by extension, individual groups) should trump any other considerations in setting social policy. The rhetoric of rights, in fact, has become the lingua franca of political life in our time – that is, of identity politics. Among those other considerations, however, are the *competing* rights of other individuals, of other groups, and of society as a whole. In this case, the second and third categories are involved. We will discuss this more fully in due course. For the time being, we draw your attention merely to the prevalence of this assumption. It is so prevalent, indeed, that many people are truly shocked when anyone suggests that redefining marriage is not simply a matter of civil rights for gay people.

> Many people are truly shocked when anyone suggests that redefining marriage is not simply a matter of civil rights for gay people.

Emotionalism: Likewise, many people now assume that the law (and much else besides) should be evaluated and legitimated primarily on emotional grounds. Its ultimate purpose, and that of the state itself, is apparently to make people feel good about themselves. Whether anything makes sense on intellectual or moral grounds is another matter. Consider *The Myth of Moral Justice*, by Thane Rosenbaum.[2] The author's main point is that courts worry too much about thinking and not enough about feeling; the legal system should be transformed, therefore, according to therapeutic principles. Although Rosenbaum is an American lawyer, we have no reason to suppose that many of his Canadian counterparts "feel" otherwise. Consider also the recent ruling on gay marriage by an Ontario court. Justice Robert A. Blair found that the evidence presented by opponents of gay marriage "does not reflect the same personal poignancy as that of the Applicants."[3] By now, politicians know that they can win support by claiming to "feel your pain" (as President Clinton did) or win sympathy by offering emotional apologies for misconduct (as Svend Robinson, among the leading lights of Canada's New Democratic Party, did more recently).[4] This mentality has been fostered for thirty years at the popular level, especially on daytime talk shows. It has been fostered also at the elite level by forms of feminism that glorify emotional warmth as something innately female (and deplore rational coldness as something innately male).[5]

Social constructionism: Many people now assume that gender and the family can be explained adequately as nothing more than "social constructions." By this, they mean that these and other institutions were created entirely by (sinister) political forces. The corollary is that these institutions can be, should be, deconstructed and reconstructed at will. This perspective has been popular for decades among some feminist and gay activists and is heavily supported by postmodernists.[6] Early feminists such as Betty Friedan argued that men and women are almost interchangeable and therefore that women should be allowed to do everything that men were allowed to do.[7] With that in mind, some feminists went one step further, arguing that women are autonomous – which is to say, that women do not need men. Taking that to its logical (and possible though not yet recognized universally as desirable) conclusion would mean creating completely[8] segregated or separate communities for each sex, thus reversing the massive cultural effort of every human society at all times and in all places.

Infinite flexibility: Because of social constructionism, many people assume that society is infinitely flexible and therefore that our society (unlike any other) can "have it all." Even now, we are losing the ability to provide public cultural support for heterosexual bonding. This would become official with the legalization of gay marriage. At best, marriage (between men and women) would be nothing more than one "lifestyle choice" among many supposedly equal ones. Any attempt to promote it for the good of society as a whole – that is, at least partly, to ensure demographic continuity – would be denounced as discrimination against gay people. It would not be merely "politically incorrect," therefore, but illegal as well.

All societies have found it necessary to establish norms,[9] which we define as cultural ideals – models, paradigms, collective preferences – that are supported by rules. This is because *no* society can have it all, just as no individual can. Every society must make *choices*. And choosing one thing – one form of behaviour, say – inevitably means not choosing others. This lies at the very heart of culture and therefore of human existence.

Because nature itself does not enforce norms, culture must do so. Every society has found it necessary – whether formally or informally, directly or indirectly – to reward some forms of behaviour and either not reward or punish others.[10] The mechanisms have varied a great deal from one society to another and from one period to another even within the same society. Small-scale societies often rely on group control: Act this way, and you will be shunned by society; act that way, and you will be honoured by society. Large-scale societies usually find it necessary to add individual control: Act this way, and you will be guilty even if not publicly condemned; act that way, and you will be justified even if not publicly acclaimed.

To the extent that norms affirm some forms of behaviour but not others, they are indeed discriminatory. But is every form of discrimination evil? No society could allow that murder, for example, is just another "lifestyle" and thus acceptable in a context of "diversity" or "pluralism." We discriminate against murder, because the collective good requires us to do so. That is an extreme example, to be sure. In our opinion, gay relationships are neither evil nor neurotic. Even so, we see no compelling reason for the state to promote them. It *does* have a compelling reason to promote straight relationships, on the other hand, in the form of marriage: to support the latter's five universal and fundamental functions (which we will discuss below). But our point here is that just because norms establish a majority, does not necessarily entail the persecution of minorities. Otherwise, no liberal democracy could exist. More about that, too, in due course.

The Defining Features of Marriage[11]

Comparative research on the worldviews of both small-scale societies and those of world religions, both Western and Eastern, reveals a pattern:[12] Marriage has universal, nearly universal,[13] and variable features.

Its *universal* features include the fact that marriage is (a) supported by authority and incentives; (b) recognizes the interdependence of men and women; (c) has a public, or communal, dimension; (d) defines eligible partners; (e) encourages procreation under specific conditions; and (f) provides mutual support not only between men and women but also between them and children.

Its *nearly universal* features are (a) an emphasis on durable relationships between parents; (b) mutual affection and companionship; (c) family (or political) alliances; and (d) reciprocity between young and old. Most large-scale societies have encouraged durable relationships between biological parents and children[14] at least until the latter reach maturity. That is because of the long time it takes infants to mature; cooperation is necessary to ensure their survival. Most societies have recognized that these are fragile bonds and therefore preferred arranged marriages (although they usually encourage affection and companionship[15] as well).

These universal and nearly universal features rely on the distinctive (but not necessarily innate) contributions of both sexes, allow the transmission of knowledge from one generation to another, and create not only "vertical" links between the generations but also "horizontal" ones between allied families or communities.

As for the many *variable* features of marriage, these include endogamy (marrying within a group) or exogamy (marrying outside it); monogamy or polygamy (and, if the latter, polygyny or polyandry); marrying up in status or marrying down; arranged marriage or chosen; dowry (from the bride's family) or bride price (goods given or services performed by the groom); sexual equality or hierarchy; many children or few; extended family or nuclear; residence with the bride's family, with the groom's, or neither; divorce allowed or prohibited; and so on. Alternatives to marriage are celebrated in some societies (as in the case of celibate monks, for instance, or shamans) and tolerated in others (such as single people or gay couples), but only when the larger society is in no danger of failing to reproduce itself.

From one perspective, variables make any definition distinctive. From another perspective, though, they create a problem. Focusing on the definition of marriage in any *one* society makes it difficult to know which aspects are distinctive or local and which are universal or nearly universal. Patterns emerge only when many societies are compared. When only one society is considered, in other words, variables can *mask* universals. We can detect universals only by using cross-cultural and historical methods. From these perspectives, as we say, patterns do emerge.

It could be argued that focusing on these universal or nearly universal features would lead to the methodological problem of "essentialism" (reductive generalization). But that is a false problem for three reasons. First, there really is an empirical basis for their existence. Second, using inductive reason to discern patterns is a fundamental characteristic of scholarship. And third, any phenomenon so common as to be universal or nearly universal surely reveals something basic in the human condition.

From all this, it should be clear that every human society has actively *encouraged* bonding between the sexes (although some have allowed bonding within the sexes, too, in various circumstances). This is directly related to both reproduction and communal survival; our species reproduces sexually, after all, which has an evolutionary advantage over the asexual reproduction of some other species.

Much of what is accomplished in animals by nature (often known as "biology," "genetics," or "instinct") must be accomplished in humans by culture (which includes not only elite culture and popular culture but all aspects of human existence aside from those that are determined by nature). Although no particular culture is genetically encoded, the universal ability and need to create culture *is*. We are equipped and even driven by nature to be cultural beings. This has made us more flexible than animals, which rely entirely (or almost entirely in the case of a few non-human primate species) on nature. And this, in turn, has greatly

> *Although no particular culture is genetically encoded, the universal ability and need to create culture is.*

facilitated our adaptation to new circumstances or environments and thus fostered human survival.

So, heterosexual bonding involves much more than copulation. It is *not* merely a given of nature for straight people. It must indeed be deliberately fostered and supported by a distinctive *culture* and always has been. Most men and women will surely continue to copulate with each other, no matter what. Whether they will remain with each other and serve the larger needs of society, well, that is another matter entirely.

In short, culture is not a thin veneer that we apply to something more primitive and basic. On the contrary, it is a defining and therefore fundamental feature of human existence. If it were somehow removed, the result would not be a functioning organism, whether human or non-human. Apart from any other handicap would be its inability to reproduce successfully. Why? Because copulating, governed primarily by nature, is not synonymous with reproduction. The latter, governed primarily by culture, includes a wide range of complex behaviours that are required by family life within a larger society.

In our view, there is nothing wrong with homosexual bonding. There is something wrong, though, with the idea that any society can endure without public support for heterosexual bonding. Every society has maintained the cultural mechanisms that provide it. These have always been associated with public legitimacy (represented by ancestors, deities, myths, scriptures, laws, and so forth), public recognition (such as rituals,[16] witnesses, and registrations), and thus public accountability. It has always been fostered by inducements, whether social (prestige, say, or political alliances), economic (transfer of property), religious (divine rewards, and so on), or a combination of them. So deeply embedded in consciousness are these that few people are consciously aware of them. The result, in any case, is a "privileged" status for heterosexual bonding. Postmodernists are correct in identifying it as such, but they are wrong in assuming that any society can do without it.[17]

The culture of marriage must encourage at least five things: (a) the bonding between men and women that ensures their cooperation for the common good; (b) the birth and rearing of children, at least to the extent necessary for perpetuating society; (c) bonding between men and children so that men are likely to become active participants in family life;[18] (d) some healthy form of masculine identity (based on the need for at least one distinctive, necessary, and publicly valued contribution to society – which is especially important today, because two of the three cross-cultural definitions of manhood, provider and protector, are no longer distinctive now that women have entered the public realm); and (e) the transformation of adolescents into sexually responsible adults – that is, young men and women who are ready for marriage and the beginning of a new cycle.

The Alleged Precedents for Gay Marriage[19]

No society has eliminated the norm of marriage (between men and women). Some societies have allowed exceptions to that norm, but the marital norm for every society has always been heterosexual.[20] Research on the history and anthropology of "gay marriage," so far, has been done mainly with advocacy in mind: supporting it by finding precedents for it. According to academic standards, this material reveals several important substantive and methodological flaws.

Some precedents are ambiguous, for instance, because they are merely analogies to marriage. Gay love is said to be *like* marital love, an initiation ritual into same-sex warrior bonding is said to be *like* marriage, and so on. Other precedents are taken out of context. It is true that some Amerindian societies allowed men to marry other men, but (judging from the information that has been recorded) these societies made sure that only a few men were allowed to do so or that their husbands had already married women and produced children so that communal survival was not endangered. Many precedents are irrelevant, moreover, because they refer only to gay *relationships*, which are not the same as marriages. And sometimes, precedents are merely implied. This is what happens when arguments are made from silence (lack of evidence meaning that something either might or might not exist) or when important information is ignored (such as the subsequent banning of marriages between people of the same sex).

The Possible Effects of Gay Marriage

Redefining marriage to include gay couples amounts to an unprecedented social experiment. The most egregious consequences would not be obvious immediately. People would not riot in the streets. Not everyone would even notice the results. Most of these, in fact, would amount at first to nothing more than continuations of tendencies already present. But in the long run, after several generations, these would bring about a radically different kind of society. Many gay and feminist revolutionaries in our own time would applaud that prospect, no doubt, but many others – including liberals who have nothing more than equality in mind – would not. The latter would do well, therefore, to consider the possible effects on us all.

The possible effects on children: At first glance, it would seem that gay marriage and gay parenting would symbolically strengthen the bonds between all parents and children. On closer examination, though, that possibility looks much more dubious. It should be clear to everyone by now that advocates of gay marriage are interested primarily or even only in the interests of (gay) *adults*. This is inadequately disguised by disclaimers. Yes, some gay people want children enough to make use of surrogacy or other reproductive technologies. And yes, some gay people have children anyway from straight relationships. But the primary focus of gay marriage would still be on adults, not children (which is why some advocates of gay marriage try to argue that children would be better off with good gay parents than with bad straight ones – even though comparing the best of one thing with the worst of another makes no sense).

> *It should be clear to everyone by now that advocates of gay marriage are interested primarily or even only in the interests of (gay) adults.*

The social-science evidence is sometimes ambiguous, moreover, but we do know by now that two parents are better for children than one[21] and that families with both mothers and fathers are generally better for children than those with only mothers or only fathers.[22] We know also that biological parents usually protect and provide for their children more effectively than non-biological ones.[23] That these facts are either ignored or trivialized by some advocates of gay marriage – and also of single parents, by the way, whether gay or straight – says something about concern for children in our time.

The possible effects on boys and men: Our inability to create and support a healthy form of masculine identity has already become a major social problem. Consider the high rate at which young men, unlike young women, not only drop out of school but also commit suicide.[24] We need no fortune teller to see that massive social problems, much more widespread than the ones we already have, are likely to emerge whenever and wherever young men are unable to feel deeply involved in family life – or, to put it another way, in the *future of society*. Over the past few decades, we have seen the re-emergence of machismo in popular culture. It now takes a particularly disturbing form: a refusal to accept the responsibilities of mature manhood.[25] To many boys and men now, it seems clear that even a *negative* identity is better than no identity at all. This alone should give us pause in contemplating the future. Because fatherhood is the one remaining source of a healthy masculine identity – and we define the latter, once again, in connection with at least one distinctive, necessary, and publicly valued contribution to society – legalizing gay marriage could leave men with a major problem.[26] We are referring specifically to lesbian marriages, which would legitimate the already widespread notion that fathers are unnecessary.

If gay people are going to have children of their own (as distinct from adopted ones),[27] it will be necessary for them to make use of reproductive technologies. These technologies will become more accepted than they are now, because demand for them will increase. The gay demand for marital inclusiveness would almost certainly include their demands for reproductive inclusiveness. It would become very easy on political grounds for male couples to argue that they are "differently situated" when it comes to reproduction and therefore demand that the *state* provide them with reproductive services such as government-sponsored surrogacy or ex-utero technologies. Failure to provide these could lead to charges of systemic discrimination against gay men, especially in view of the fact that Bill C-6, *An Act respecting assisted human reproduction and related research*,[28] would discourage surrogacy by forbidding potential surrogate mothers to accept payment for their services.[29]

And gay men would be by no means the only ones to make reproductive demands. The door would be open to other men seeking reproductive autonomy through technology. Straight men could well come up with demands of their own. Many already believe that marriage, even common-law marriage, is becoming too risky in view of current laws governing divorce, custody, and child support. Why not redefine the family with their own interests in mind? Why not demand access by single men, for instance, to surrogacy?

But the problem for men goes even further. For the past several decades, feminists have campaigned for reproductive autonomy and power – for women, of course, not for men. More and more straight single women are choosing to have children but not husbands.[30] If women but not men have reproductive autonomy, then both gay and straight men will be increasingly marginalized from reproduction. So far, every culture has encouraged cooperation between men and women through marriage. Women have gained not only protection but also resources for themselves and their children. Men have gained not only status but also a healthy source of identity. This exchange, based on interdependence, would be destroyed by any culture that promotes reproductive autonomy for women but not men. If we can learn anything from history and evolution, it is surely that men are unlikely to give up on either personal or collective reproduction – which is to say, on active participation in the most universal and fundamental project of society: continuity. More men than ever would resort to transitory sexual encounters with women.

If women but not men have reproductive autonomy, then both gay and straight men will be increasingly marginalized from reproduction.

Men would be the big losers, in short, because both gay and straight women would have much easier access to reproduction than gay or straight men (unless someone solves the problem of biological asymmetry by inventing an artificial womb – and governments introduce the appropriate legislation).

The possible effects on women: According to *Women and Men Unglued,*[31] a documentary produced by the National Film Board of Canada, many young people no longer expect (although they might still want) to have durable marriages; some are not even sure about transient "relationships." The reason, says Barbara Whitehead, is that neither sex believes that it needs the other (even though that belief is harder for men to substantiate than it is for women). Men and women come together now and then, if at all, for purely physical or emotional reasons. But the film indicates that many of them, especially women with ticking "biological clocks," want children anyway. These women could turn to other women for emotional and financial support, especially if they were allowed to marry. And that would send an even more powerful message: that men have no fundamental importance in family life. This message, already common but not yet given official approval by the state, would be a big problem for women who still value men in their lives and the lives of their children.

The possible effects on single people: The main premise of those who demand gay marriage is not that marriage confers financial or legal benefits, because these could be attained just as easily through benefit packages or civil unions, but that marriage confers self-esteem or dignity. If that were so, then one implication would be that single people cannot – perhaps should not – have self-esteem or dignity. Single people have always been treated with condescension (especially single women) or suspicion (especially single men). Instead of solving that problem, those who demand gay marriage would exacerbate it. Or, to put it another way, they would solve the problem for themselves by imposing it even more harshly on others. Single status would be even more marginal than it already is. As some gay people have pointed out, albeit with their own collective self-interest in mind, redefining marriage to include gay people would actually increase the level of conformity rather than create a truly "diverse" society.

Redefining marriage to include gay people would actually increase the level of conformity rather than create a truly "diverse" society.

The possible effects on society: At the heart of this campaign for gay marriage is, as we have already said, radical individualism (coupled, ironically, with a form of radical collectivism).[32] We are not referring to the kind of individualism that emerged in the eighteenth century and was expressed most effectively by those who wrote the American Constitution. For them, individual liberty was embedded firmly in a context of communal responsibility. In short, personal liberty was not synonymous with personal licence. Today, individualism has come to mean something quite different, something that approaches the adage that "anything goes" (as long, presumably, as no one is personally injured). The larger interests of society no longer function as constraints. And this indifference to society as a whole is made clear by those who demand gay marriage. Allowing gay people to marry, they say, would be beneficial to gay people, both individually and collectively. How could that harm straight people, they ask, whether individually or collectively? But they have made no serious attempt to consider the possible harms.

Whatever might be said about the immediate consequences of radical individualism, the long-term consequences could be dire. One scenario would be the dissolution of society as such, as a unified whole. It would devolve into a collection of adult individuals focused exclusively on their own rights as individuals and tolerating governance by society only as a way of protecting these from other individuals.[33] More specifically, in connection with redefining marriage, men and women would come together for copulation and companionship, but enduring bonds would be seen as unnecessary restrictions on personal freedom. Their children would be either shunted from one home to another, depending on arrangements made primarily to suit the changing desires of adults, or reared in institutions run by the state. Marriage has never before been so heavily associated with the wants and needs of adults as individuals. On the contrary, it has always been associated primarily with the needs of children (expressed as the ideal of interdependence between men and women for the sake of children) and the needs of society (expressed as the ideal of interdependence between men and women for the sake of society as a whole).

The "philosophy" that underlies radical individualism is hedonism. By that, we refer not to the mere affirmation of personal pleasure but to the glorification of personal pleasure as an end in itself. Drug addiction, to take only one example, is also not a result of poverty and ignorance. It is a fashion, a "lifestyle." Hollywood stars move in and out of rehab as often as they move in and out of marriage. And they are applauded for talking about it to Oprah Winfrey.

Gay people did not invent hedonism. Although gay people are sometimes associated with hedonism,[34] for instance, this mentality had never been unknown to straight people and is now at least as pervasive among them as it is among gay people. Nor did gay people invent radical individualism. Although they have adopted it successfully, this political strategy had already become pervasive in the straight world. The campaign for gay marriage was inconceivable, in fact, until both hedonism and radical individualism had already come to prevail in the larger society. The chickens have come home to roost, as it were, and straight people have only themselves to thank for any dire consequences.

The possible effects on religious communities: Canada welcomes immigrants, many of whom are religious. But religious freedom would become increasingly difficult to defend. Even if exceptions were initially made for religious officials, not forcing them to marry gay couples, these exceptions would almost certainly be challenged in the courts. The latter would have to choose between two competing rights: freedom of religion versus equality. Guess which one is likely to trump the other?

The Canadian Human Rights Commission is already intervening with the Supreme Court (presumably on behalf of those who advocate gay marriage) on the government's *Marriage Reference*, even though the United Nations has not supported same-sex marriage.[35] And several cases suggest that the courts are already willing to privatize religion or restrict the values of religious institutions. We will discuss these in the next section, though, because they indicate the possible effects on education as well.

The possible effects on education: In *Trinity Western University* v. *British Columbia College of Teachers*,[36] the Supreme Court overruled a lower court that had tried to prevent a religiously affiliated institution's teacher-education program from being certified by the province because of that institution's views and policies on homosexuality. Certification was allowed, because the "proper place to draw the line [between freedom of religion and freedom from discrimination] is generally between belief and conduct. The freedom to hold beliefs is broader than the freedom to act on them."[37] No evidence had been offered that graduates of Trinity were likely to act in a discriminatory fashion when teaching in public schools, by condemning homosexuality or disapproving of homosexuals.

Consider also *Chamberlain v. Surrey School District No. 36*.[38] The school board refused to add three books to its list of supplementary books for classroom use at the elementary level; each was about a family headed by two parents of the same sex. The Supreme Court ruled that the school board must revisit this decision, arguing that the curriculum should acknowledge impartially all points of view and therefore promote equality.

The principles at work in these two cases suggest that the problem is not only one of religious freedom. A worrisome tendency to privatize religion is accompanied by a tendency to suppress public debate. The supposed celebration of diversity, in the name of tolerance, simply ignores the fact of *conflict* between competing worldviews and the resulting conflict between competing views of family and marriage. Students need (at an appropriate age) to discuss and debate these conflicts, giving due consideration to etiquette, in order to understand the society in which they live. But if the courts are willing even now to privatize and possibly marginalize religion, and to include gay families in books for six-year-olds, then we should expect the curriculum in public schools in the immediate future to include gay marriage and the courts to punish teachers for discrimination if they present nonconformist views in class. And the same scenario will be repeated in universities despite our vaunted academic freedom.[39] All this amounts to state-sponsored social engineering on the basis of a state-supported ideology – which is tantamount to an official state religion.

> *A worrisome tendency to privatize religion is accompanied by a tendency to suppress public debate.*

The possible effects on democracy: Finally, consider democracy. In one way, the campaign for gay marriage seems to support democracy. Its rallying cry is that gay citizens should have the same rights, after all, as other citizens. In another way, though, it undermines democracy – which involves both majorities and minorities, by definition (everyone being part of a majority in some ways and of a minority in other ways). Liberal democracies do protect minorities from any tyranny of the majority, but the reverse should be true as well. Advocates of gay marriage are confused. They want to be a proud minority but also, paradoxically, *not* to be a minority. They want to be different from the majority, in other words, but not to pay a price for being different. And there is always a price (no matter how minimal) for being different (no matter which way). If minority status itself becomes intolerable, if the very fact of difference is said to be inherently degrading and destabilizing, then how can we sustain a democracy, let alone a "pluralistic" one?

Tolerance and Wisdom

Not every society fosters heterosexual bonding *effectively*. Our own ideal is hardly the current status quo, in which the marriage licence has been reduced by irresponsible straight people to nothing more than the proverbial "piece of paper" at worst and pure sentimentality at best. For evidence of the latter, just take a cursory glance at such massively popular television shows as *The Bachelor*, *The Bachelorette*, and *Joe Millionaire*. Participants, who hope to marry as a result of appearing on the show, seldom talk about anything more serious than how they like to spend their free time, whether to reveal their feelings, or, occasionally, how many children they would like to have. They never ask prospective husbands or wives about political beliefs, say, or communal affiliations. For them, courtship and marriage, like the show itself, are forms of entertainment. Careful attention to sets – lavish hotel suites, exotic locales, dozens of candles everywhere – creates the "romantic" ambience of a soap opera. Although ritualistic aspects remain – the most obvious being when a young man kneels as he proposes marriage – many of these are anachronistic, to say the least. This nonsense is (or has been until recently) manufactured and sold primarily by and for straight people, not gay people.

> *No one can predict the future of this experiment. People are not rats in a lab.*

No one can predict the future of this experiment. People are not rats in a lab. Unforeseen things are just as likely to happen because of social engineering as they are because of any other kind, only mistakes in a social experiment are much more costly. We try to fix every problem, but we usually end up replacing one with another. Thirty-five years ago, it seemed like common sense that changing the divorce laws would be an act of compassion for the few but one that would make little or no difference to the many. That was naïve, to say the least; we know better now. It changed us in ways that no one could have imagined. For better or worse – better for some, worse for others – we now live in a "divorce culture."[40]

Nevertheless, we will almost certainly be accused of alarmist rhetoric. Given the historical record of societies in the midst of major changes, though, we could refer to even more alarming possibilities. Remember that every morally responsible analysis of social policy must include consideration of the *risks*. Naïveté, like cynicism, is hardly a virtue.

Most people like to consider their society a tolerant one, and this is certainly laudable. But no society could endure if tolerance were taken to its ultimate conclusion: the belief that "anything goes." In addition to tolerance – otherwise known as "love," "caring," or "compassion" – every society must be guided by *wisdom*. And that requires citizens to be as reasonable as they are tolerant. Canadians should think twice, therefore, before redefining marriage.

Notes

1 In cases of discrimination, the legal test starts with section 15(1) of the *Charter* where the person alleging discrimination must establish the facts that support this. If the court finds that there is discrimination, the defendant can turn to section 1 as a defence. That requires the defendant to prove that the discrimination is justified within the terms of section 1. In short, those opposing same-sex marriage would have the section 1 burden of proof.

2 Thane Rosenbaum, *The Myth of Moral Justice: Why Our Legal System Fails to Do What's Right* (New York: HarperCollins, 2004).

3 *Halpern v. Canada (A.G.)*, [2002] 60 O.R. (3d) 321 (Ont. Div. Ct.) [hereinafter *Halpern*] at para. 5, Blair J.

4 Robinson stole an expensive ring and returned it after realizing that he had been caught on video. Weeping at a press conference, he attributed his behaviour to stress (and, later, to post-traumatic stress disorder due to an accident that had occurred seven years earlier). Robinson decided to leave office temporarily, but won accolades in the press for his exceptional courage and "honesty."

5 See Paul Nathanson, "I Feel, Therefore I Am: The Princess of Passion and the Implicit Religion of Our Time" in *Implicit Religion*, 2.2 (1999): 59–87.

6 See Daphne Patai, *Heterophobia: Sexual Harassment and the Future of Feminism* (Lanham, MD: Rowman and Littlefield, 1998).

7 They did not care that this notion of equality ignored a biological asymmetry, women being able to do at least one thing that men cannot do.

8 See Patai. Many societies have sexual segregation in one form or another (longhouses for men, convents for women, and so on) but always place sexual segregation within a larger (reproductive) framework.

9 See Katherine K. Young, affidavit for *Halpern*, supra note 3, along with *EGALE Canada* v. *Canada (A.G.)* [2001] B.C.S.C. 1365, and *Barbeau* v. *British Columbia (A.G.)*, 2003 BCCA 251.

10 In an ideal world, we would support marriage as a privileged estate. In the real world, however, we recognize the need for compromise. The current debate forces Canadians to choose between equality and family. Taken to its logical conclusion, the former would support gay marriage; the latter would oppose civil union. Our position is a mediating one. We oppose gay marriage but support civil union. We define civil union as a legally recognized relationship between adults. It signifies to the community that they are willing to care for each other socially and economically. It provides legal mechanisms for doing so. In addition, it protects each party if the union is dissolved.

11 This section is based on Young's affidavit for *Halpern*, supra note 9, with minor changes.

12 For definitions of marriage based on comparative evidence, see Susan G.E. Frayser, *Varieties of Sexual Experience: An Anthropological Perspective on Human Sexuality* (New Haven, CT: HRAS Press, 1985), p. 248; G. Robina Quale, *A History of Marriage Systems* (New York: Greenwood Press, 1988), p. 2; and Edith Turner and Pamela R. Frese, "Marriage," in Mircea Eliade, ed., *Encyclopedia of Religion*, vol. 9 (New York: Macmillan, 1987), p. 218.

13 Major civilizations include both universal and nearly universal features, which is why both categories must be considered in connection with the modern societies that emerged from them.

14 Because of the time it takes infants to mature, cooperation is necessary to ensure their survival. As a result, most societies have encouraged durable relationships between biological parents and children at least until the latter reach maturity. In some small-scale societies, however, the community distributes resources to everyone and assigns everyone the responsibility of protecting the young; durable relationships between biological parents are less important, therefore, than they are in large-scale societies (where the family is the basic social unit). But most people live in large-scale societies, such as ours, so durability is as important as the universal features.

15 Most societies have recognized that mutual affection and companionship facilitate bonding between men and women, but others have recognized that these are fragile bonds and therefore have preferred arranged marriages.

16 Among Orthodox Jews, for instance, all men are expected to marry. Only *married* men are entitled to wear the *tallit* (prayer shawl). Something similar is true of Hinduism. Most Hindu men have had to marry, although a few exceptions have been allowed. We could give dozens of other examples. Our point is that the use of culture in this way could be construed as "privileging" heterosexuality and therefore be attacked as "politically incorrect."

17 Sexual orientation is *not* entirely a "social construction" and therefore subject to eternal deconstruction and reconstruction. Heterosexuality has a partially biological foundation in most people, for instance, but nonetheless functions effectively only when *fostered* by religious or other cultural institutions. In other words, important aspects of it must be taught within a larger cultural context – more specifically, within a moral one. But some scientific evidence suggests that homosexuality, too, might have a partially biological foundation. (In *Adam's Curse: A Future Without Men* [New York: Norton, 2004], Bryan Sykes examines the evidence for a "gay gene" and concludes that the "concordance rates for male homosexuality certainly do indicate some degree of genetic influence" [p. 260]. See his discussion of the evidence on twins, the size and structure of the amygdala, the influence of sex hormones in fetal development, and so on [pp. 254–73].) We do not believe that gay people should be harmed by cultural guidance provided for the majority. Therefore, we argue that cultural institutions, including religious ones, should avoid negativity toward the gay minority even as they support the straight majority. Many have already taken steps to do so.

18 Traditionally, every society has used symbols and rituals to foster the bonding between men and children. One reward for Jewish fathers, for instance, is being able to participate in rituals with their sons. Examples include *brit milah* (circumcision on a son's eighth day), *pidyon ha-ben* ("redeeming" a first-born son, on his thirtieth day, by replacing him with a monetary donation to the "Temple"), and *bar mitzvah* (the first time that he is called to read the Torah in synagogue). Indebted to the ancestors, Hindu men are obliged to have sons who will perform their funeral rituals later in life. Although this created the problem of son preference, its underlying raison d'être was to give men a heavy investment in family life.

19 Young's affidavit for *Halpern*, supra note 9, with minor revisions.

20 It is worth noting that any society *could* have used culture to encourage gay marriage and still reproduce itself. Women could always have found ways of procuring sperm, for instance, and men could always have abducted children or hired surrogates. But this approach has never been adopted as a norm.

21 As single parents know, the time and money of two adults are better than those of only one.

22 We are embodied beings, and our bodies are (with very rare exceptions) either male or female. Feminists have been arguing for decades that no man can teach any girl or woman about the experience of being female, but that insight applies equally in reverse: no woman can teach any boy or man about the experience of being male. (In each case, they can teach children some useful things but not everything.) Children learn much by way of example. With this in mind, advocates of gay marriage often point to surrogate models of the opposite sex. But these are by no means universally available or even as available as they once were. Many mothers have brothers and fathers who live far away. Not all of their boyfriends, moreover, are eager to become surrogate fathers (because that task involves a high level of altruism). Most teachers of young children are still women. And as for the men that children see on television, not many are worthy of emulation – for more on that, see Paul Nathanson and Katherine K. Young, *Spreading Misandry: The Teaching of Contempt for Men in Popular Culture* (Montreal: McGill-Queen's University Press, 2001) – and none could be emulated anyway in the intimate and enduring context required by children. To learn about their own bodies, children need at least one parent of the same sex. To learn about the culture of heterosexuality –

and most children, though not all, are inclined to become heterosexual – they need at least one parent of the opposite sex as well; what they learn is mainly a result of how their mothers and fathers interact.

23 Because of the emphasis today on supporting adoptive parents and single parents (especially those who have been forced into this situation by unfortunate circumstances), many people now hesitate to mention the importance of biological parents. But social scientists have shown that children not living with both of their married biological parents are at a greater risk of physical and emotional abuse. See M. Daly and M.I. Wilson, "Some Differential Attributes of Lethal Assaults on Small Children by Stepfathers versus Genetic Fathers" in *Ethology and Sociobiology* 15 (1994): 207–17; M. Daly and M.I. Wilson, "Violence Against Stepchildren" in *Current Directions in Psychological Science* 3 (1996): 77–81; C.D. Siegel at al., "Mortality From Intentional and Unintentional Injury Among Infants of Young Mothers in Colorado, 1982 to 1992" in *Archives of Pediatric and Adolescent Medicine* 150.10 (1996): 1077–83. Evolutionary psychologists have shown also that men are more likely to provide for their children if they know that they are biologically related. See Don Browning, *Marriage and Modernization: How Globalization Threatens Marriage and What to Do About It* (Grand Rapids, MI: Eerdmans, 2003), pp. 75–76.

24 For the suicide rates of men and women, see *2001 Annual Report* (Ottawa: Statistics Canada, 2002): 46; see also Elizabeth Thompson, "Québec Leads Provinces in Suicides: Rate Among Our Men Is More Than Triple That of Québec's Women, Study Finds," *Montreal Gazette*, 18 Sept. 2002, p. A14. For the school dropout rates of men and women, see "Labour Force Statistics" [undated], *B.C. Stats* [visited] 3 Oct. 2002, www.bcstats.gov.bc.ca.

25 That is because our society has failed to articulate any vision of mature manhood that satisfies the needs not only of women but also of men themselves. Say what you like about earlier versions of machismo, at least they were based on a glorification of manhood rather than of boyhood. John Wayne exemplified an ideal that involved emotional withdrawal, true, but he exemplified in addition one that involved service to the community and even self-sacrifice (especially in times of conflict or war). Today, the Farrelly brothers and other filmmakers like them present us with the cinematic ideal of men who are really adolescent boys (preoccupied with sexual games) or even preadolescent boys (preoccupied with body functions and toilet humor). A rare exception is *Master and Commander: The Far Side of the World* (Peter Weir, 2003), which represents traditional machismo (and not only because of its eighteenth-century setting). Both male protagonists, the dutiful and compassionate "master and commander" along with his gentle and intellectual friend, are truly worthy of emulation.

26 See David Blankenhorn, *Fatherless America: Confronting Our Most Urgent Social Problem* (New York: Basic Books, 1995); Chris Coughlin and Samuel Vuchinich, "Family Experience in Preadolescence and the Development of Male Delinquency" in *Journal of Marriage and the Family* 58.2 (1998): 491ff; George Thomas and Michael P. Farrell, "The Effects of Single-Mother Families and Nonresident Fathers on Delinquency and Substance Abuse" in *Journal of Marriage and the Family* 58.4 (1996): 884ff.

27 Despite liberal adoption laws in the West, they would find it hard to adopt children from other countries; the latter usually prefer to place children with straight (married) couples.

28 3rd Sess., 37th Parl., 2004. This bill received royal assent on 29 March 2004, after this essay had been written.

29 According to its statement of principles, Bill C-6 says that "while all persons are affected by these technologies, women more than men are directly and significantly affected by their application and the health and well-being of women must be protected in the application of these technologies" and that "persons who seek to undergo assisted reproduction procedures must not be discriminated against, including on the basis of their sexual orientation or marital status." Thus, if it is argued (and it has been) that paid surrogacy and artificial wombs are detrimental in any way to women's well-being, including their identity, then these technologies would be illegal.

The bill would ban surrogacy explicitly and artificial wombs implicitly. Although lesbians have encouraged gay marriage for men, they could (and probably would) argue against their use of paid surrogates or artificial wombs because of the need to protect women's reproductive interests against those of men – even those of gay men, despite the hype over discrimination on the basis of sexual orientation. The bill would prevent payment for both sperm and eggs, but it would not make sperm banks and egg banks illegal.

To find out in more detail what is in store, read *Proceed With Care: Final Report of the Royal Commission on New Reproductive Technologies* (Ottawa: Minister of Government Services Canada, 1993). Sperm donors would be compensated only for their inconvenience and for the direct costs of donation (recommendation 88(k); vol. 1, p. 477). But given the low cost of sperm in any case, this is a moot point; the real problem is presented by egg banks. Sperm collection and distribution facilities would be licensed by the government (recommendation 84; vol. 1, p. 478). "Sperm [would] be provided to individual women for self-insemination without discrimination on the basis of factors such as sexual orientation, marital status, or economic status" (recommendation 94 (f), vol. 1, p. 480). Finally, the "use of imported sperm [would not be] permissible" (recommendation 99(a); vol. 1, p. 484). Because the latter is readily available in American sperm banks, a growing mail-order industry, it is clear that both the Royal Commissioners and the authors of Bill C-6 are serious about giving Canadian *women* full reproductive autonomy.

30 See Tamala M. Edwards, "Flying Solo," *Time*, 28 Aug. 2000, pp. 36–43.

31 Katherine Gilday, *Men and Women Unglued* (Ottawa: National Film Board of Canada, 2003).

32 We refer not to nationalism, which is about society as a whole, but to what is often called "identity politics." Underlying the demand for individual rights is a *qualification* that usually remains hidden by political or ideological rhetoric: that this is about rights for the individuals of specific *groups*. The debate over gay marriage, for instance, is ultimately about *gay* rights, not merely individual rights. But the rhetoric of individual rights, per se, has become our legal lingua franca.

33 Closely related to that scenario is a more extreme (but by no means impossible) one: anomie. That word refers literally to the absence of law. In a larger sense, it refers to the absence of social cohesion and sense of collective purpose. We have already referred to social fragmentation. The signs of social decay, at least the early warnings, are everywhere in Western countries. Consider only the high rates of divorce, the millions of abandoned wives and fatherless children, and the prevalence of addictions. Not one of these problems, *alone*, is likely to destroy a

society. But so many problems, most of them closely linked, should give us pause before redefining so basic an institution as marriage.

34 Even the gay people who do conform to stereotypes of gay behaviour have also been among those most actively involved in altruistic behaviour on both the personal level (caring for partners with AIDS) and the communal (lobbying for more research on AIDS and more public services for those who have AIDS).

35 See the *Canadian Human Rights Commission, Annual Report*: 2003 (Ottawa: Minister of Public Works and Government Services, 2004) and the United Nations International Covenant on Civil and Political Rights (ICCPR), Article 23, which upholds the "right of men and women of marriageable age to marry and to found a family").

36 [2001] 1 S.C.R. 772 [hereinafter *Trinity*].

37 Ibid. at 2. [Editors' note: There is a fuller treatment of both these cases in the essay in this volume entitled "Whose Rights? Whose Freedoms?"]

38 [2002] 4 S.C.R. 710.

39 One of us (Young) has already been subjected to intimidation because of an abstract of her proposed affidavit along with that of Margaret Somerville. See Lisa Fitterman, "McGill Profs Square Off Over Same-Sex Marriages," *Montreal Gazette*, 3 Feb. 2003, pp. a-1-2; Joslyn Osenberg, "Same-Sex Marriage Debate Comes to Campus: Campus Activists Condemn Two McGill Profs Testifying Against Queer Couple," *McGill Daily*, 29 Jan. 2001, p. 2. If this occurred over an abstract, imagine the chill on academic freedom and research grants on this topic if the state were to decide that any opposition to gay marriage amounts to unfair discrimination.

40 Barbara Dafoe Whitehead, *The Divorce Culture* (New York: Knopf; Random House, 1997).

WHAT ABOUT THE CHILDREN?

What About the Children?

Margaret Somerville

"Questions are not neutral" is a truism in ethics. The questions we choose to ask, and not to ask, frame an issue and its ensuing debate and, thereby, often have a major impact on our responses to that issue.

The main question so far in the same-sex marriage debate is: Is it discrimination to exclude same-sex couples from marriage? Advocates of same-sex marriage and the courts (except the trial court in British Columbia) have answered yes. But there is another equally important question that can be used to frame the debate, and that is: What are the rights of children? The answers to this further question may cause us to respond differently to the first question regarding discrimination, as compared with how we respond to that question when it is asked alone or seen as primary.

Do children have a basic right to know who their biological parents are and to be brought up by them? Does society need an institution that establishes that right as one of its basic principles and norms? If our answers are "yes," then we must say "no" to changing the definition of marriage to include same-sex couples.

Across millennia and societies, marriage has institutionalized and symbolized the inherently procreative relationship between a man and a woman. It has established the societal norm that in entering marriage a man and a woman take on shared obligations to protect and nurture the children born to them. The corollary of those adult obligations is a child's right to know and to be brought up by his or her biological parents, unless an exception can be justified as in a child's best interests. Same-sex marriage would radically change that norm.

Same-sex marriage presents a difficult choice between conflicting claims, each of which can be characterized as a right. It is true that same-sex marriage would be an important affirmation of respect for homosexuals and a public recognition of the wrong of discriminating against them. But it would also, unavoidably, be a societal declaration that children don't have any basic right to know who their biological parents are and that they don't need both a mother and a father. Same-sex marriage makes children's rights secondary to adults'. It contravenes the ethical principle that children, as the most vulnerable people, must come first.

It is important to understand that it makes a major difference with respect to children's rights in general whether non-traditional families are seen as within the norm or as an exception to it. Norms, in contrast to exceptions, set basic rules or presumptions. Including same-sex families within the norm means that children do not have a basic right to know and be brought up by their biological parents. That is not true if such families are seen as a justifiable exception to the norm.

And there is also a very important ethical difference between society establishing an institution that of its nature deprives children of their right to a mother and a father, and that situation arising because of the choices of individuals, whose choices, for reasons of privacy and respect, should not be interfered with. While society would have ethical obligations not to interfere with the freedom of individuals in relation to reproduction (subject to restrictions on the use of reproductive technologies, discussed below), it also has obligations not to facilitate the creation of situations that are not in the "best interests" of children. In short, the compliance – and even more so the positive assistance – of society in helping to create non-traditional families in which children will be reared is not an ethically neutral act. This means that such compliance or assistance must be justified, or, more precisely, that the breach of children's rights involved must be justified.

Advocates of same-sex marriage do not, however, usually provide such justification for the breach of children's rights that same-sex marriage would entail – probably because to do so would be to recognize that these rights exist and also, perhaps, because adults' claims that their rights have justified priority over children's rights seem, at best, deeply selfish. Rather, they deny that these rights exist (the most common approach) or ignore them. Or, if they do recognize them, they simply assume that they are justified in not honouring them.

To the proposition that children need and have a right to both a mother and a father, same-sex marriage advocates respond by arguing that, with divorce and children being born outside marriage and to single women, marriage often doesn't achieve its goal of ensuring that a child knows and is brought up by its biological parents: so why worry that same-sex marriage would eliminate the norm that marriage establishes in that regard? However, like democracy, the issue is not whether marriage, as it stands, is a perfect institution, but whether society and especially children are better off with it than without it. As well, to buttress their arguments, same-sex marriage advocates compare failed examples of traditional marriage in relation to caring for children with the best examples of doing so in non-traditional families. But that is not a fair or accurate assessment.

Advocates of same-sex marriage also argue that they love their children just as much as opposite-sex parents love their children – or even more, because all their children are "planned and wanted." But, important as it is, love is not the only important element in a child's life. To intentionally disconnect children from their biological parents, or from access to the knowledge of who those parents are – and therefore who the children are – is a very serious action that requires strong justification, especially when the action is facilitated by society.

So what basic presumptions should govern us as a society in our treatment of children? And when there is conflict between what adults want and what children need, who should be given priority?

When there is conflict between what adults want and what children need, who should be given priority?

It may be politically incorrect to say so, but I believe that a child needs both a mother and a father and, unless there are good reasons to the contrary, is best off being reared by his or her own biological mother and father. We can see the deep human need to be connected to our origins through the intense desire of adopted children – and, more recently, of those born from donated sperm or ova – to find their birth parents. Defining the institution of marriage as the union between a man and a woman is our recognition as a society of those needs of children to be connected to their biological origins and reared by their biological parents and our way of trying to ensure that those needs are fulfilled. And marriage is unique among societal institutions in doing that; there are no alternatives. Same-sex marriage would mean that marriage could no longer perform those tasks because marriage could no longer symbolize and institutionalize the inherently procreative relationship between a man and a woman from which their children result.

Should marriage be primarily child-centred or adult-centred?

The crucial question is: Should marriage be primarily a child-centred institution or an adult-centred one? The answer will decide who takes priority when there is irreconcilable conflict between the best interests of a child and the claims of adults. Opposite-sex marriage does not raise this question because, within it, adults' claims and children's needs are consistent. That is not true of same-sex marriage.

Those who believe that children need and have a right to both a mother and father, preferably their own biological parents, oppose same-sex marriage because, as explained above, it would mean that marriage could not continue to institutionalize and symbolize the inherently procreative capacity between the partners; that is, it could not be primarily child-centred.

Those who believe that marriage is primarily about two adults' commitment to each other support same-sex marriage. They focus on the identical nature of the commitment between the partners in a same-sex marriage and an opposite-sex one, to establish discrimination in excluding same-sex partners from marriage. This argument for same-sex marriage is primarily adult-centred.

The same is largely true of the arguments of same-sex marriage advocates with respect to bringing children into their relationships. They speak of their rights not to be discriminated against in doing so. When the matter of children's rights and best interests is raised, they justify their stance with arguments that a child is no worse off – or is even better off – with same-sex parents than opposite-sex ones. They reject a child's need for complementarity in parenting – the combination of the different kind of parenting given by a mother and a father. As an aside, that rejection contrasts with the feminist critique of the law, which is based on the profound difference between a male and female approach to law. It would seem that the law needs complementarity, but children do not.

In short, accepting same-sex marriage necessarily means accepting that the societal institution of marriage is intended primarily for the benefit of the partners to the marriage, and only secondarily for the children born into it. And it means abolishing the norm that children – whatever their sexual orientation later proves to be – have a prima facie right to know and be reared within their own biological family by their mother and father. Carefully restricted, governed, and justified exceptions to this norm, such as adoption, are essential. But abolishing the norm would have a far-reaching impact.

What is the connection between same-sex marriage and reproductive technologies?

The new reprogenetic (reproductive and genetic) technologies also raise questions relating to same-sex marriage. One response that many have given, including the Canadian courts in their rejection of arguments that marriage should be restricted to opposite-sex couples because only they can procreate, is that same-sex couples can now use reproductive technologies to bring children into their marriages. Future possibilities could include making an embryo from two sperm so that two men could have a baby, or from two ova so that, likewise, two women could have their "own" child. If it is discrimination to exclude same-sex couples from marriage, then surely it would be an even more serious instance of discrimination to prohibit them from reproducing in the only way possible for them as couples. If so, could some of the prohibitions in the new *Assisted Human Reproduction Act*, which recently received royal assent, be challenged constitutionally on discrimination grounds? Notably, the act does prohibit discrimination in access to reproductive technologies on the basis of marital status or sexual orientation. Is the act's prohibition on paying surrogate mothers or gamete donors, thereby establishing the value that human reproduction is "not for sale," inconsistent with this anti-discrimination clause? Some feminists argue that restrictions on surrogate motherhood are justified because surrogacy demeans women and, therefore, should be restricted. In other words, they place women's rights to be respected ahead of those of gay men to found a family. But they do not do the same for children; *their* rights are secondary to those of same-sex couples.

New reproductive technologies open up a wide range of possibilities for having children. While the act does contain a prohibition on cloning, it does not prohibit making an embryo from two ova or two sperm or multiple genetic parents. Could homosexual couples argue that it is discrimination to prohibit them from creating children between them by using reprogenetic technologies in whatever way they saw fit? If their claim were upheld, it could mean that a prohibition on creating a child by cloning or the other methods mentioned above would be unconstitutional under the *Canadian Charter of Rights and Freedoms*. And such a prohibition could also offend same-sex couples' rights to found a family, rights that come with marriage as a matter of law, for instance, under the *International Covenant on Civil and Political Rights*. Yet, society must limit the use of these technologies to protect children. Moreover, both respect for the children brought into being through the use of reproductive technologies and respect for the transmission of human life, itself, require that its transmission be limited to sexual reproduction resulting from the union of an ova and a sperm.

> *Could homosexual couples argue that it is discrimination to prohibit them from creating children between them by using reprogenetic technologies in whatever way they saw fit?*

More explicitly, the combination of same-sex marriage and reproductive technologies raises concerns beyond just its impact on individual children, important as that is. In upholding respect for the inherently procreative relationship, marriage upholds respect for one particular aspect of that relationship, the transmission of human life – which is the first event in procreation. The unprecedented modes of transmission of life, described above, face us with unprecedented challenges to maintaining that respect. Marriage must remain limited to opposite-sex couples if we are to have an institution that establishes a social-sexual ecology of human reproduction that symbolizes respect for the transmission of human life through sexual reproduction, and limits its transmission to that mode, as compared with, for example, through asexual replication (cloning). There is no alternative institution.

To summarize, new reprogenetic technoscience confronts us with questions no other humans have had to address, because in the past, for example, the only mode of transmission of human life was sexual reproduction in vivo. Now we must ask: What is required for respect for the *mode of transmission* of human life to the next generation? And what is required for respect for the children who would result from the use of reprogenetic technologies to bypass nature? Our response to same-sex marriage will necessarily form part of our response to these questions.

Do the reasons for opposing same-sex marriage matter?

The reasons for excluding same-sex couples from marriage matter. If the reason for denying same-sex marriage is to show that we have no respect for homosexuals and their relationships, or to communicate the message that homosexuality is wrong, then the exclusion of same-sex couples from marriage is ethically unacceptable from the perspective of respect for homosexuals and their relationships. It is also discrimination from a legal perspective.

On the other hand, if the reason is to keep the very nature, essence, and substance of marriage intact, and that essence is to give children mothers and fathers by protecting the inherently procreative relationship, then excluding same-sex couples from marriage is ethically acceptable from the perspective of respect for them and their relationships. And such a refusal is not legally actionable discrimination.

Respect for others' religious beliefs in a multicultural society can raise complex issues. Some people object to same-sex marriage on the basis of their religious beliefs. These beliefs are often profound, and the people who hold them see a complex interplay in marriage between its voluntary formation, religious sanction, social legitimation, and natural origin. Even if we do not agree with these beliefs, indeed even more so if we do not, we need to understand what they are in order to understand the impact on the people who hold them of legally recognizing same-sex marriage. We must likewise take into account the impact on same-sex couples of refusing to recognize their relationships as marriage. We are in a situation of competing sorrows or harms.

We must ask which approach to the marriage question best accommodates mutual respect. Both sides in this debate must recognize that they can only demand respect from their opponents if they give it; that is, if respect is to be present at all, it will only be so in a context of mutual respect. To the extent that we can avoid transgressing people's religious beliefs, even though we do not agree with them, we should not transgress them, out of respect for the people who hold them, not out of respect for those beliefs. The same is true for people who oppose homosexuality on moral grounds in relation to their having respect for homosexuals, if not for their beliefs. Ethics requires us to take the least invasive, least restrictive alternative that is reasonably available and likely to be effective in achieving a justified goal. Maintaining traditional marriage and legally recognizing same-sex partnerships fulfils that ethical requirement.

Note, this same accommodation of respect for beliefs in the formation of public policy would *not* apply to beliefs, based on religion, about the wrongfulness of homosexuality. While such beliefs may be held by individuals or groups, they are not acceptable as the basis for public policy decision-making in a secular society, if only because the harm of recognizing such beliefs far outweighs the harm of not doing so. That is why opposing same-sex marriage on the basis that it involves recognizing a homosexual relationship is not valid, and why opposition on the basis that such recognition necessarily destroys the essence of marriage is valid. There is a major difference between not destroying the essence of marriage for people who will enter into that institution and whose religious beliefs mean that recognizing same-sex marriage would destroy it, and recognizing, at any public policy level, the same people's anti-homosexual beliefs. The latter is unacceptable because it directly denigrates homosexuals, rather than seeking a justified goal (maintaining marriage); and because others' sexual orientation, unlike the recognition of same-sex marriage, in no way directly affects the people who regard homosexuality as morally wrong.

One strategy used by same-sex marriage advocates is to label all people who oppose same-sex marriage as doing so for religious or moral reasons in order to dismiss them and their arguments as irrelevant to public policy. Good secular reasons to oppose same-sex marriage are re-characterized as religious or as based on personal morality and, therefore, as not applicable at a societal level. In the same vein, people who oppose same-sex marriage are labelled as homophobic, ultra-conservative, or self-righteous. These are ad hominem attacks that do not seek to address the arguments but to denigrate and thereby dismiss the people so labelled. They cause people to fear speaking out and do not serve the best interests of either individuals or society in this debate.

Should the law abandon marriage?

The use of law can never be neutral, whether we are enacting, changing, or repealing it. We use law in postmodern, secular societies such as Canada to challenge or uphold our most important societal values. Whereas, in the past, our moral and values discussions took place in religion, they now take place in our legislatures and courts. One way to regard our Parliament, legislatures, and highest courts is as the "secular cathedrals" of our society.

One of the options that have been proposed for resolving the same-sex marriage debate is that Parliament should repeal the laws on marriage and abandon the area of marriage. That would not be a neutral act. It would necessarily change the values and symbolism associated with marriage. We legislate about matters associated with our most important societal values; delegislating marriage, therefore, would detract from its importance and the values associated with it. Whether or not we agree with all of the provisions the *Assisted Human Reproduction Act*, its enactment recognizes that there is a need – both practical and symbolic – to legislate in relation to reproduction. It would be paradoxical if, at the same time, we were to delegislate marriage.

At the individual level, many young people who see no problems with sexual relationships outside marriage or with living together before marriage, do go on to get married either before having children or if pregnancy or birth occurs. This fact shows the current importance of the role of marriage with respect to the values governing procreation. We can argue that this reality makes maintaining the institution of marriage and the values and symbolism associated with it *more* necessary and *more* important than in the past, and that it requires maintaining marriage as a legal construct. Marriage is needed as a societal institution, not just a religious (quasi-private) one, to mark out and mark off the intrinsically procreative relationship from other types of relationship. If it were not available to perform these functions – which it would not be if it were redefined to include same-sex couples – there would be no societally sanctioned way that people, such as those just described, could symbolize for themselves, others close to them, and society that their relationship had changed because they were becoming or had become parents. That would be particularly true for people who were not religious.

But what about homosexuals who bring existing children into their relationships? Shouldn't these adults have access to marriage? This is the most powerful argument, in my view, for recognizing same-sex marriage, but I do not believe it justifies extending marriage to same-sex couples, for the reasons given throughout this essay in support of the traditional definition of marriage as a relationship between a man and a woman. Bringing children into a same-sex relationship should not be seen as within the norm, but rather as an exception to it. Recognizing same-sex marriage would make bringing children into a same-sex relationship part of the norm, rather than an exception. We should recognize same-sex relationships and legally protect them and any children involved, but not by recognizing the same-sex couples' relationship as marriage.

Bringing children into a same-sex relationship should not be seen as within the norm, but rather as an exception to it.

Can separate institutions be equal?

Same-sex marriage advocates reject a two-institutions – marriage and civil partnerships – approach to the recognition of committed adult relationships. They argue that separate cannot be equal – that is, that the reality of separation itself constitutes inequality. But there is a difference between separate but equal and different but equal. Separate but equal means that two entities are inherently the same but are nonetheless treated differently. That is discrimination. Different but equal means that two entities are not inherently the same but are treated equally. That is the antithesis of discrimination. Separate but equal is second-class citizenship or worse. Different but equal is not.

The question is, therefore, whether homosexual unions and heterosexual unions are inherently the same, in which case they should constitute one group of unions, or are inherently different but should be treated equally. The answer depends on which characteristics of these unions we choose to focus.

If we focus on adult individuals' commitment to each other and public recognition of that commitment (as the courts have done), we can conclude that restricting marriage to opposite-sex unions and having a separate but equal institution for same-sex unions would be discrimination. But if we focus on the inherently procreative nature of an opposite-sex union and the absence of that feature in a same-sex union, we can regard the two types of union as different but equal. Women, provided they are treated as equal to men, are not second-class citizens when recognized as women and not as men. In like manner, same-sex unions, provided they are treated as equal to marriage, are not second-class unions when not recognized as marriage.

In rejecting a two-institutions approach, advocates of same-sex marriage argue that marriage is open to change and recognizing same-sex marriage is just one more change. This raises the issue of whether marriage is simply a social construction or has some inherent natural reality to it. Social features are open to change. Inherent, natural ones are not. Marriage, like many important social institutions, is a combination of natural reality (the biology of procreation) and social construct (the culture that nurtures and supports procreation). The conventions that have traditionally surrounded marriage show this duality.

Take, for instance, the spouses' promise of fidelity. One purpose of this promise was to ensure that the husband could be certain that the children to whom his wife gave birth were his genetic progeny. (Until the advent of reproductive technologies, she could be sure they were hers.) That certainty was not only for the husband's benefit, but also for the wife's and children's. It made the husband willing to invest his resources in bringing up his children and supporting his wife. Parents' honouring of their promise of fidelity also helps to ensure a stable home life for children and allows them to know their genetic heritage. A sense of genetic identity – as many people deprived of this demonstrate – is a powerful human need.

Sexual monogamy is a given in the Western institution of marriage, though it is not always honoured in practice by individuals. In contrast, it is often stated that one of the first decisions to be negotiated between same-sex partners is whether the relationship will or will not be sexually monogamous. For gay partners, faithfulness can be a commitment to a lifelong relationship in which the fidelity is to the relationship, not to a monogamous sexual partnership. Marriage between one man and one woman, as stated in the vows, "to the exclusion of all others," symbolizes sexual monogamy. The same is not necessarily true of same-sex marriage.

Other changes in marriage that are put forward as precedents for changing marriage to include same-sex couples include the facts that husbands can no longer beat their wives with legal impunity, that interracial marriages are no longer illegal, that the partners in many opposite-sex marriages do not or cannot have children, and that divorce is no longer illegal. But these are not relevant analogies. Institutions have inherent features and collateral features. Inherent features go to the very nature and essence of the institution and define it. These features cannot be changed without destroying the institution (which, it merits noting, is sometimes warranted, but I'm assuming none of us wants to destroy marriage). Collateral features can be changed without such impact. We rightly recognized that women must be treated as equal partners to men within marriage. That changed the power of husbands over their wives – for example, husbands lost their immunity for assault. But that was to change a collateral feature of marriage: the power balance between the spouses. Recognizing same-sex marriage would be to change the inherent nature of marriage.

The argument that excluding same-sex couples from marriage is the same act of discrimination as prohibiting interracial marriage is also flawed. Interracial marriage symbolizes the inherently procreative relationship between a man and a woman; the only reason for prohibiting it, therefore, is racial discrimination. Same-sex marriage expressly and directly negates this symbolism. That, and not their sexual orientation, is the reason for denying same-sex partners access to marriage. Denying access on the basis of the former reason is not discriminatory; denying it on the basis of the latter would be.

Arguments against the central role of the procreative symbolism of marriage, based on the existence of many childless marriages, are rebuttable, too. In contrast to same-sex marriage, these marriages do not contravene the procreative symbolism of marriage at the general or societal level. Similarly, it is argued that acceptance of divorce provides justification for changing marriage to include same-sex couples. The issue is not, however, whether all or most opposite-sex couples attain the ideals of marriage; neither is it whether marriage is a perfect institution – it is not. The issue, rather, is whether society needs marriage to institutionalize and symbolize, as it has done across millennia and societies, the inherently procreative relationship between a man and a woman. Opponents of same-sex marriage believe we need this and that maintaining it should take priority. Advocates of same-sex marriage believe that recognizing homosexual people's claims to have access to marriage should come first. The conflict at the heart of this disagreement – as is so often true in ethical dilemmas – is whether societal needs or individual rights should prevail. Important as the latter are, we would do serious harm in simply assuming that they should always trump the former.

The conflict at the heart of this disagreement – as is so often true in ethical dilemmas – is whether societal needs or individual rights should prevail.

Is a separate-but-equal-institutions approach discriminatory?

Same-sex-marriage advocates claim that an approach based on two separate-but-equal institutions is discriminatory in its essence. If so, it would be unacceptable. To decide we must look first at the context in which separate-but-equal institutions are proposed; second, at whether there is a relevant difference between them; and, third, at the reasons for adopting that approach.

Rejection of a separate-but-equal approach on the grounds that it is necessarily discrimination is usually referenced to a 1954 judgment of the United States Supreme Court, *Brown* v. *The Board of Education*, without any mention of the context in which that judgment was handed down. The court concluded that "*in the field of public education*, 'separate but equal' has no place. Separate educational facilities [on the basis of race] are inherently unequal." But that is not necessarily true of establishing separate institutions in other areas, on other grounds.

In particular, it is not necessarily true of institutions for the public recognition of committed adult relationships, when, as is true for marriage and civil unions, they encompass different realities and carry different symbolism. Indeed, it is not even true of all separate educational institutions. Separate schools for girls and boys – separate, that is, on the basis of sex and not race, as in the *Brown* case – can be equal and are not seen as discriminatory by most people, even though sex, like race, is normally a prohibited ground of discrimination. That is because reasons can determine whether a given act is discrimination.

Take the example of allocating shared hospital rooms. Allocating shared rooms on the basis of race would be discrimination, but doing so on the basis of sex is not. Indeed, failure to do the latter can be a breach of a person's human rights and dignity. The family of a very old woman who died in a room shared with a young man is still traumatized by their mother's deep distress at finding herself in this situation – she had never been in bed in a room with a man present other than her husband or a physician. In short, the same act can be discrimination or not, depending on the reasons for undertaking it. Although normally we regard separating men and women as discrimination, in this poor woman's case, failure to do so was a failure of respect.

Should we equate homosexuality to race or to sex in the above examples when deciding on a one- or two-institutions approach to same-sex unions? The central issue in that decision, as those examples show, is: What is required in terms of respect? Some reasons for undertaking an act mean that it manifests respect, other reasons for the same act mean that it shows disrespect.

I have argued that to reject same-sex marriage in the public square in order to affirm moral or other objections to homosexuals is a failure of respect and would be discrimination. To reject it because marriage could no longer embody the inherently procreative relationship between a man and a woman and, thereby, institutionalize and symbolize the functions of marriage related to procreation and children would not be discrimination. Many – one hopes the vast majority – of opponents of same-sex marriage do not disrespect homosexuals or their relationships. Yet the same-sex marriage case is based almost entirely on equating being against it with being against homosexuals, disrespecting them, and thereby breaching their human rights. That connection needs to be challenged.

And respect is not a one-sided issue. Same-sex marriage raises fundamental issues of *mutual* respect, something that often goes unrecognized by its advocates. What is required to respect homosexual people and their committed partnerships, *and* to respect people for whom marriage institutionalizes and symbolizes the inherently procreative relationship between a man and a woman? The only "least invasive of both streams of respect" response is to legally recognize same-sex partnerships and keep marriage as the union of a man and a woman. However, same-sex marriage advocates reject that option outright.

Same-sex marriage raises fundamental issues of mutual respect, something that often goes unrecognized by its advocates.

Is it a breach of human rights to reject same-sex marriage?

Many same-sex marriage advocates seem to have their facts wrong with respect to a central claim on which they base their argument that opposing same-sex marriage is a breach of human rights. They claim that the *International Covenant on Civil and Political Rights* (ICCPR) supports same-sex marriage as a human right. In fact, it does the opposite.

Article 23 – the right of men and women to marry and found a family – is the only right in the Covenant phrased in terms of men and women. All the other provisions articulating people's rights use the word "everyone." Under normal rules of statutory interpretation, this shows an intention to make a distinction between the attribution and exercise of other rights and the right to marry. The only possible distinction is that men and women have a right to marry, but men and men and women and women do not, at least pursuant to this provision. This interpretation was affirmed recently by the United Nations Human Rights Commission (UNHRC), which decided that the ICCPR does not confer a right to marry on same-sex couples. The case was a same-sex marriage challenge from New Zealand. In 1997, the New Zealand Court of Appeal held in *Quilter* v. *Attorney General* ([1997] ICHRL 129) that the New Zealand *Bill of Rights*, which unlike the Canadian *Charter* expressly prohibits discrimination based on sexual orientation, does not require recognition of same-sex marriage. A complaint against this judgment to the UNHRC was rejected by it in 2002.

The Best Interests of the Child

It is important to identify the context in which comments on same-sex marriage are grounded, because in this debate context is definitely not neutral and is not the same for everyone. Some who oppose extending the definition of marriage to include same-sex couples do so on religious grounds or because of moral objections to homosexuality. In contrast, my arguments against same-sex marriage are secularly based and, to the extent that they involve morals and values, are grounded in ethics not religion.

To summarize: First, I oppose discrimination on the basis of sexual orientation, whether against homosexuals or heterosexuals. Second, I believe that civil partnerships open to both opposite-sex and same-sex couples should be legally recognized and that the partners, whether opposite-sex or same-sex, are entitled to the same benefits and protection of the law. But, third, I believe that we should not change the definition of marriage to include same-sex couples.

My reasons go to the belief that children need and have a right to both a mother and father and (unless some other arrangement can be justified as in the best interests of a particular child) a right to know and be reared by their own biological parents. Restricting marriage to the union of a man and a woman establishes that right of children as the societal norm. In other words, it is a fundamental purpose of marriage to give children both a mother and a father, preferably their own biological parents. Changing the definition of marriage to include same-sex couples would overtly and directly contravene both the right and the norm and would mean marriage could no longer function to affirm the biological bond between parents and their children.

In short, marriage, as it stands, is the societal institution that represents, symbolizes, and protects the inherently reproductive human relationship for the sake of children born of such relationships. Society needs such an institution and marriage is unique in this regard; there is no other alternative.

WHOSE RIGHTS? WHOSE FREEDOMS?

Whose Rights? Whose Freedoms?

Darrel Reid and Janet Epp Buckingham

Everyone has the following fundamental freedoms:
(a) freedom of conscience and religion;
(b) freedom of thought, belief, opinion and expression . . .

– Canadian Charter of Rights and Freedoms

When the concept of gay marriage was merely a polling question dropped into the middle of an otherwise enjoyable dinner, Canadians paid the issue little attention. But when the government began to promote the file, moving the issue closer to public consciousness, Canadians began to voice their concerns. A good many of those concerns revolve around questions of religious freedom, and that ought not to surprise us. The great majority of Canadians are religious adherents of one sort or another,[1] and many of them see Canada's new social experiment as a real threat to their religious communities and to their way of life. When same-sex marriage is discussed as an issue of rights and freedoms, the question that frequently arises is: *Whose* rights? *Whose* freedoms?

The broader impact of the gay-rights agenda was already a matter of concern in the 1990s, and ad hoc coalitions were formed to contest parts of that agenda.[2] Awareness of a budding conflict with religious rights was still largely restricted to religious leaders, however, and to interest groups concerned about religious freedom or freedom of expression.

But alarm began to spread with the growing ambition of the gay-rights movement in the courts and in Parliament. Beginning in the year 2000, cases in British Columbia, Ontario, and Québec were orchestrated by EGALE (Equality for Gays and Lesbians Everywhere) with the direct aim of redefining marriage. Like Svend Robinson's much-contested Bill C-250, which called for the addition of the words "sexual orientation" to Canada's hate-propaganda legislation, these eventually met with complete success.

There was some astonishment on all sides at the speed of this black-robed revolution. Until very recently, Canadian courts saw themselves as upholders of the traditional order, partly because they recognized the value of stable marriages and the benefits they provided to families. Even though gay groups were making good progress in achieving marriage-related benefits through the courts, marriage's foundations remained clear to jurists. This was stated most eloquently by Justice La Forest in 1995, in a passage that bears repetition:

> Marriage has from time immemorial been firmly grounded in our legal tradition, one that is itself a reflection of long-standing philosophical and religious traditions. But its ultimate *raison d'être* transcends all of these and is firmly anchored in the biological and social realities that heterosexual couples have the unique ability to procreate, that most children are the product of these relationships, and that they are generally cared for and nurtured by those who live in that relationship. In this sense, marriage is by nature heterosexual. It would be possible to legally define marriage to include homosexual couples, but this would not change the biological and social realities that underlie the traditional marriage.[3]

What a difference a few short years make! By the time the Ontario Court of Appeal handed down its ruling on *Halpern* v. *Canada*, this view had been turned completely on its head. According to the court, marriage (so conceived) was suddenly arbitrary and indeed discriminatory. The entire institution therefore required fundamental, court-imposed change: "It is our view that the dignity of persons in same-sex relationships is violated by the exclusion of same-sex couples from the institution of marriage. Accordingly, we conclude that the common-law definition of marriage as 'the voluntary union for life of one man and one woman to the exclusion of all others' violates s. 15(1) of the *Charter*." And the remedy for this constitutional infringement? "We . . . declare the existing common-law definition of marriage to be invalid to the extent that it refers to 'one man and one woman.'"[4]

The news that marriage was inherently discriminatory came as a shock to most Canadians, the overwhelming majority of whom do not accept the courts' new view of the matter.[5] Even more of a shock was the federal government's announcement, on 17 June 2003, that it would drop its defence of the common-law definition of marriage. This, more than any other single event, galvanized the popular opposition. People across the country were roused from their slumbers and became intensely interested in what redefinition could mean to them, their families, their churches, and their communities. Front and centre among their concerns were issues related to children and the education of children, and behind that the issue of religious freedom on which all such questions eventually come to rest.

Of course, religious-liberty concerns were well known to the federal government. It had heard them repeatedly through the years in which the gay-rights agenda was being advanced, through many court interventions – in several of which religious groups and government lawyers cooperated – and through the government's abortive Justice Committee hearings on same-sex marriage in 2002 and 2003. Clearly, religious objections were a major strategic hurdle for the government.

> *Clearly, religious objections were a major strategic hurdle for the government.*

What to do? When Jean Chrétien and Martin Cauchon announced that the government would not appeal the *Halpern* decision, they immediately assured Canadians that the government was deeply concerned with religious freedom and freedom of conscience, as well as with equality rights for gays. The former would be guarded by guaranteeing in law that clergy would not be forced to marry same-sex couples against their religious beliefs. Given that 97% of marriages in Ontario, Canada's most populous province, are performed by clergy, this was not merely a cosmetic consideration. It was repeated, mantra-like, at every opportunity in the ensuing weeks and months. When on 17 July 2003 Mr. Cauchon announced the government's intention to seek the Supreme Court's opinion on its approach to same-sex marriage, it was there: "We need an approach that applies across the country and recognizes the equality of all Canadians. At the same time, the government of Canada must ensure that freedom of religion – another fundamental Canadian value – is equally respected. I believe the draft bill strikes the right balance."[6]

Canada's religious groups did not respond as hoped, however. The Evangelical Fellowship of Canada, a leading voice in the Interfaith Coalition opposing same-sex marriage, observed: "We are deeply concerned that the effect of the redefinition will be to begin a process of marginalization for many churches and their clergy who currently participate in the civil registration of marriage."[7] Canada's religious leaders had expected to have their concerns about religious freedom, and the concerns of their constituents, taken into account in a serious manner. That the federal government felt it had done so, by means of this single provision, only indicated to them how badly flawed was its concept of religious freedom, and how recklessly inadequate was the legislation it had proposed.

Reckoning With Religious Freedom

From the *Québec Act, 1774* to the establishment of Ontario's public-school system, concern for religious freedom has never been far from the surface of public life. Thus the 1960 *Bill of Rights* and the 1982 *Charter of Rights and Freedoms* gave constitutional recognition to a well-established fact. According to the latter, everyone has as the first of his or her fundamental freedoms, "freedom of conscience and religion," and in addition – as a natural extension, we might say – "freedom of thought, belief, opinion and expression."

Not surprisingly in a constitutional democracy, these concepts have been given meaning by the courts. Until recently, Canada's courts have recognized what every person of sincere faith knows instinctively, that freedom of religion is not just the right to assent to a series of propositions privately. After all, even the most despotic regimes of the twentieth century had no problem with that. Rather, freedom of religion means allowing an individual the widest possible scope within which to act on those views and to communicate them with others, whether in the home, the workplace, the school, or the public square. In the first case on the issue to come before the Supreme Court of Canada, known as the *Big M Drug Mart* case, Chief Justice Dickson established the nature of religious freedom in broad terms:

> The essence of the concept of freedom of religion is the right to entertain such religious beliefs as a person chooses, the right to declare religious beliefs openly and without fear of hindrance or reprisal, and the right to manifest belief by worship and practice or by teaching and dissemination . . .
>
> Freedom means that, subject to such limitations as are necessary to protect public safety, order, health, or morals or the fundamental rights and freedoms of others, no one is to be forced to act in a way contrary to his beliefs or his conscience.
>
> What may appear good and true to a majoritarian religious group, or the State acting at their behest, may not, for religious reasons, be imposed upon citizens who take a contrary view. The *Charter* safeguards religious minorities from the threat of "the tyranny of the majority."[8]

What shall we make, in this light, of the federal government's assertion that it will protect religious freedom by including in the proposed legislation a provision that clergy shall not be required to perform ceremonies contrary to their religious beliefs? That provision has always been in place, of course, and merely to reiterate it is not even to begin to address the reality of the new legal situation.[9] What exactly has changed to make it necessary to reaffirm this provision or to restate this principle? Is the principle itself somehow at odds with the new legal situation? If so, how well and how long can this provision stand up under the pressures that the new situation will bring to bear on it?[10]

It is, in any case, a remarkably thin view of religious freedom that is satisfied by this single protection. Clergy, after all, are not the only ones who solemnize marriages. Presumably, a great many judges, justices of the peace, and marriage commissioners have religious beliefs also. How will they be accommodated – or will they? Already the British Columbia government has laid down an ultimatum to its 301 marriage commissioners. They were required to resign if they did not find it possible to solemnize same-sex marriages. Whatever justification may be offered for such an ultimatum, its effect is clear enough. Those with strong religious convictions – or at least those with religious convictions that conform to the near-unanimous position of the major Western religions that there can be no such thing as same-sex marriage[11] – will be drummed out of this important public-sector vocation.

But even that consideration does not take us to the heart of the matter. The fact is that millions of Canadians who are opposed to same-sex marriage have now been told by the courts that their view on marriage is contrary to the *Charter* and, by extension, un-Canadian. This pits the *Charter*, which is meant to protect freedom of religion and conscience, *against* their consciences and indeed their religions, and that on a fundamental matter. Meanwhile, the proposed federal legislation redefining marriage offers not a shred of protection for religious adherents, their clergy, or their institutions, beyond the single limited provision already noted.

> *The proposed federal legislation redefining marriage offers not a shred of protection for religious adherents, their clergy, or their institutions, beyond the single limited provision already noted.*

The consequences of all this remain to be seen, though they have already been hinted at in various places. In Ontario, for example, during the debate over the Equity in Education tax credit,[12] one member of the provincial parliament argued strenuously that schools which, as he put it, teach discrimination against gays and lesbians should not be beneficiaries of the tax credit. This took direct aim at Christian, Jewish, and Muslim schools.

The Uneven Playing Field

Over the past several years, case after case has pitted gay rights against religious freedom. Some of these cases have gone all the way to the Supreme Court of Canada; human-rights tribunals have decided others. All of them lead to the inexorable conclusion that the courts have dramatically reversed their former understanding of the nature and depth of religious conviction.

The Supreme Court of Canada set up an interesting approach to dealing with the gay-rights-versus-religious-freedom conflict in two cases in British Columbia. The first involved a Christian university, Trinity Western University, which was trying to get approval for its teacher-education program. The university was turned down by the accreditation body, the British Columbia College of Teachers, because the college was concerned that the university's "community standards" document would lead teachers graduating from Trinity Western to be discriminatory against gays and lesbians. The College appeared to be concerned about putting the stamp of approval of the state on a university that practised discrimination against gays and lesbians. It compared Trinity Western University with Bob Jones University in the southern United States, from which the U.S. government withdrew benefits because the university was discriminatory on the basis of race.[13]

The Supreme Court of Canada was not persuaded by the "race card." Rather, the court would interpret the rights of both sides so that there was no conflict between them. In this case, the court delineated the rights as follows: Christian students have the right to go to a university and assent to religious practices that are discriminatory, but once they are out in the non-religious world, they must refrain from discrimination. The education program was approved.[14]

The court went on to apply this approach in a second case, this one involving the Surrey School Board, which had refused to approve storybooks featuring same-sex parents for use in kindergarten and grade-one classrooms. The school board based its refusal largely on the concerns of religious parents. The court ruled that religious parents have every right to express their concerns about approval of books. But (and here is the catch) religious concerns cannot be used to exclude another group. So, religious parents can go to a board of education and express concerns that books featuring same-sex parents contravene religious teachings and will confuse young children, but the board cannot act on those concerns because to do so would exclude from the classroom materials about same-sex parents. The result is readily apparent, and religious parents may as well stay home.[15]

While the Supreme Court has stated clearly that there is a "level playing field" of rights – that is, that no right is superior to another – the way the court has interpreted religious freedom and gay rights leaves gay rights in a superior position. In the Trinity Western University case, the court said that the "freedom to believe" is broader than the freedom to act on those beliefs. Respecting gay rights, however, the courts have ruled that protection for homosexual practices is part and parcel of the protection for "sexual orientation." Justice L'Heureux-Dubé, dissenting in the Trinity case, argued that "the status/conduct or identity/practice distinction for homosexuals and bisexuals should be soundly rejected."[16]

Clearly, if homosexual practices are protected without question but religious practices are subject to some more rigorous standard, gay rights will always trump religious rights.

Clearly, if homosexual practices are protected without question but religious practices are subject to some more rigorous standard, gay rights will always trump religious rights. But of even greater concern is the way courts are presuming to act as judges of religious beliefs and practices. The most egregious example is that of Marc Hall,[17] a gay student at a publicly funded Ontario Roman Catholic high school. Directly contrary to the teaching and doctrine of the Catholic Church, Hall decided that he wanted to bring his gay partner to the school's prom. The school and the school board had told the young men not to participate, because Catholic teaching, which at the school all students are expected to obey, prohibits homosexual behaviour. It should go without saying that Catholic teaching provides the fundamental underpinning of the Catholic school system. The judge, however, ignored the testimony of the local bishop. He ruled that there was not unanimity among Catholics about issues of homosexuality, as though the Catholic Church were a democracy. In effect, the judge presumed that he was better qualified to determine Catholic doctrine and practice than the Pope, the bishops, or the local Catholic school board. On what basis? And what is the point of having separate Catholic schools if they cannot enforce Catholic teachings on important subjects like sexual morality?

Religious-rights advocates have also watched with growing concern a series of rulings, arising from the application of provincial human-rights codes, that, taken together, point toward the constriction of religious freedoms.

In 2002, the Ontario Divisional Court upheld a ruling by an Ontario human-rights tribunal that a business owner could not refuse to provide services to an organization even if the organization's fundamental purpose violated his religious conscience.[18] Scott Brockie is a Toronto printer who refused to print letterhead and stationery for the Canadian Lesbian and Gay Archives. Brockie is an evangelical Christian. The Archives promotes homosexual history, identity, and culture. The promotion of homosexual behaviour is a cause that offends Brockie's conscience. The court ruled that if Brockie's right to religious freedom were recognized in allowing him to refuse to provide services in this situation, the whole of human-rights legislation would be undermined. Rather than take this dangerous step, it offered a narrower acknowledgement of his religious beliefs: Brockie could (only) refuse to print materials the content of which actually offended his beliefs. Meanwhile, he was fined for offending the dignity of his gay-rights accusers.

Later in 2002, the Saskatchewan Queen's Bench ruled that an ad containing Bible verses violated prohibited hate speech under a human-rights-code provision.[19] Hugh Owens had published an ad in the Saskatoon *Star-Phoenix* newspaper to coincide with Gay Pride Day in Saskatoon. The ad contained the following list of biblical references: Romans 1, Leviticus 18:22, Leviticus 20:13, and 1 Corinthians 6:9–10. This was followed by a graphic of two stick men holding hands, superimposed on which was a circle with a slash through it, the universal symbol for "Do not do this." In response to a complaint, the Saskatchewan Human Rights Commission ruled that this ad, intended to express God's displeasure with homosexuality, in fact incited hatred toward homosexuals. When the case was appealed to the courts, Justice Barclay upheld the judgment, writing: "In other words, the Biblical passage which suggests that if a man lies with a man they must be put to death exposes homosexuals to hatred." According to the judge, under certain circumstances, the Bible can constitute hate literature.

According to the judge, under certain circumstances, the Bible can constitute hate literature.

Also in 2002, the B.C. College of Teachers disciplined public-school educator Chris Kempling – an exemplary teacher with a tremendous reputation and many commendations – for conduct unbecoming a teacher, giving him a one-month suspension. His crime? Writing letters to the editor and an opinion piece in his local newspaper, expressing concerns about a "gay-friendly" curriculum to be introduced into the schools. The truly chilling part of this story is the fact that the college sanctioned Kempling for writing an opinion piece in a newspaper – a freedom that should be granted to every citizen. Kempling appealed to the B.C. Supreme Court, but the court upheld the sanction.[20] Justice Holmes ruled that the constitutional protection for freedom of religion and freedom of expression did not apply to Kempling in this case. Justice Holmes even ruled that the famous section 15 of the *Charter*, the anti-discrimination provision, did not apply because Kempling could not prove that he was treated differently from any other teacher in British Columbia.

Connecting the dots of these cases led one analyst, Iain Benson, to comment that Christians will soon inhabit the closets so recently vacated by gays.[21]

A Question of Trust

Given recent signals from the courts, and the government's own record on same-sex marriage, can its assurances about religious liberty be trusted? Clearly there are grounds for skepticism. Recall, for example, the assurances offered by (then justice minister) Anne McClellan during a 1999 debate on marriage in the House of Commons:

> Let me state again for the record that the government has no intention of changing the definition of marriage or of legislating same sex marriages. No jurisdiction worldwide defines a legal marriage as existing between same sex partners . . . The definition of marriage as a union between one man and one woman is found in the common law of our country and the common law of our system of law. It is also found in the civil law of the country . . . We [the government] thought perhaps we could spend our time debating other issues as opposed to that on which there is clarity in the law.[22]

This was with respect to the motion, which passed by a large majority, requiring the federal government to take "all necessary steps" to preserve the traditional definition of marriage. Needless to say, when this motion was reintroduced by the opposition in September 2003 – after the courts' and the federal government's *volte-face* – McClellan reversed her earlier vote. With her help, the motion was defeated by a slim majority. Is it any wonder that religious communities are fearful about the protection of their religious freedoms in the wake of the redefinition of marriage?

They have been made even more fearful by the recent passage of Bill C-250. Just as the courts were ruling that marriage as traditionally defined was an inherently discriminatory institution – and suggesting that people who continued to support it were intolerant and homophobic – there, making its way through Parliament, was a bill that actually held out the possibility of criminal sanctions against such people.[23] It is the very vagueness of this bill's provisions, and its faint hint of menace, that deeply concerns Canada's religious leaders. For, given what we have been hearing from our courts and human-rights tribunals, it is not a stretch to see *Criminal Code* sanctions being brought to bear against individuals proclaiming their religious views about sexual morality or same-sex marriage.

True, this bill contains a defence for "good faith . . . opinion on a religious subject." But courts and human-rights tribunals have been interpreting this so narrowly that it is difficult to see the phrase as anything more than an attempt to soothe the consciences of human-rights activists intent on dragging before their tribunals Canadians brave enough to read the Bible in public, or to speak on the basis of their religious convictions.[24] The Evangelical Fellowship of Canada, in its opposition to C-250, put it thus: "What confidence can we have that the defences will be sufficient to allow the public expression of moral and religious views on a variety of sexual practices? We are concerned that adding sexual orientation to s. 318 of the *Criminal Code* will put a chill on legitimate religious expression concerning sexual practices."[25]

Religious communities also anticipate more subtle, but still serious, forms of attack. We have mentioned already, among other things, the threat to charitable status and tax exemptions. But what about their buildings, for example? At least one Roman Catholic church has received inquiries about rental of the parish hall for the reception of a same-sex marriage. A dispute over rental of a Manitoba church camp might also be cited. In this case, a gay man has brought a complaint to the Manitoba Human Rights Commission because his group was refused use of the camp. It is not yet known whether the commission will recognize the church's right to refuse to offer its facilities to groups whose beliefs and practices are antithetical to its own.

Something Must Be Done

Most Canadian religious communities agree that marriage is an institution fundamental to society: that it is rooted in the divine order of the universe and yields unique benefits to human beings and to the body politic. These communities are not able, nor are they willing, to redefine marriage simply because the courts say that this primordial institution has become – suddenly and capriciously – contrary to *Charter* values.

Is religious freedom, as it is being interpreted by the courts in Canada, sufficiently robust to protect religious citizens and institutions from misguided policy-makers and from the legal assaults of their opponents?

But is religious freedom, as it is being interpreted by the courts in Canada, sufficiently robust to protect religious citizens and institutions from misguided policy-makers and from the legal assaults of their opponents? The Supreme Court of Canada has set out its interpretation of religious freedom in high-blown phrases but has proven more than able to reverse course under contrary winds, especially when it comes to gay rights. And it is from precisely this quarter, if the lower courts and the human-rights tribunals are anything to go by, that the greatest threat to religious freedom presently comes.

Something must be done. There is already growing evidence that Canada's social contract, that tacit agreement among citizens to support the state in return for having their freedoms respected and defended, is beginning to fray. This can be seen, for example, in the steady stream of people making their exodus from the public-school system. Should ordinary religious Canadians become persuaded that their most deeply held beliefs and values are indeed irreconcilable with public policy under the current *Charter* regime, that stream could turn into a torrent.

The fact is that Canada's public square – the place where people of all faiths and walks of life meet, work, study, debate, play, and worship – is becoming a colder, lonelier, and less welcoming place. Canadians of all faiths would do well to pray that this trend will be arrested and reversed quickly for the good of their families, their communities, their churches, and their nation.

Notes

1 If there is one value shared by the vast majority of Canadians, it is their adherence to their religious heritage and identity. The 2001 Canadian census reveals that almost 84% identify with one of the world's major religions, and predominantly with Christianity: Roman Catholic (43.2); Protestant (29.2); Christian Orthodox (1.6); Christian, not included elsewhere (2.6); Muslim (2.0); Jewish (1.1); Buddhist (1.0); Hindu (1.0); Sikh (0.9); no religion (16.2). (See Statistics Canada's 2001 census analysis series, *Religion in Canada*, p. 18.) This tallies with the results of a recent Ipsos-Reid poll (15 Oct. 2003), in which 71% of Canadians agreed with the statement, "I believe Jesus was crucified, died and was buried, but was resurrected to eternal life."

2 An Interfaith Coalition on Marriage and Family, including the Evangelical Fellowship of Canada, Focus on the Family, the Islamic Society of North America, the Ontario Conference of Catholic Bishops, and the Ontario Council of Sikhs, intervened in the 1995 case *Egan* v. *Canada*, [1995] 2 S.C.R. 513 [hereinafter *Egan*] and *M.* v. *H.* (1999), 43 O.R. (3d) 254 (S.C.C.). These organizations also formed coalitions to intervene in the marriage cases across the country.

3 *Egan*, supra note 2.

4 *Halpern* v. *Canada (A.G.)*, (2003) O.A.C. 172 at paras. 108, 156 [hereinafter *Halpern*].

5 According to a COMPAS poll, 8 Dec. 2003, 63% of Canadians support retaining the traditional, heterosexual definition of marriage. Thirty-one percent are in favour of redefining marriage, and 6% remain undecided.

6 "Minister of Justice Announces Reference to the Supreme Court of Canada," Department of Justice Statement, 17 July 2003. Irwin Cotler, Mr. Cauchon's replacement as minister of justice, stated "that the Government of Canada is reaffirming its position in the marriage reference, organized around two foundational principles – support for equality – and within that the extension of civil marriage to same-sex couples – and support for religious freedom – and within that protection for religious officials from being forced to perform a marriage ceremony between two persons of the same sex where it is against their religious beliefs." "Government of Canada Reaffirms Its Position on Supreme Court Reference," Department of Justice Statement, 28 Jan. 2004.

7 "EFC Is Disappointed in No-Appeal Decision on Marriage," EFC Press Release, 17 June 2004.

8 *R.* v. *Big M Drug Mart*, [1985] 1 S.C.R. 295 at 336–37.

9 Cf. Douglas Farrow and David Novak, *National Post*, 31 Jan. 2004, p. A7: "That protection for clergy even requires consideration speaks volumes about

the illiberal character of [the government's] legislation, and about the threat it poses both to freedom of religion and freedom of speech."

10 The provision itself has notable weaknesses. First, the power of "solemnization of marriage" rests with provincial governments, not the federal government. Second, the legislative provision drafted to "protect" clergy religious freedom is framed in the negative. It does not grant positive protection.

11 These religions regard marriage as a universal norm rooted in a divinely constituted order that preconditions law and politics. Marriage, in other words, is not at bottom a social construct, the fundamentals of which may be changed at will. It is by nature a heterosexual institution, which has procreation within its purview. It does not and cannot have homosexual conduct, which in Western religions is regarded as unacceptable, within its purview. See further the affidavits of Abdallah Idris Ali, Daniel Cere, Craig Gay, David Novak, and John Witte, Jr., filed on behalf of the Interfaith Coalition on Marriage and Family, in *Halpern* v. *Canada (A.G.)*, [2002] 60 O.R. (3d) 321 (Ont. Div. Ct.) [hereinafter *Halpern* (2002)].

12 This tax credit was available to defray the cost of private-school education in Ontario. It has been repealed.

13 *Trinity Western University* v. *British Columbia College of Teachers*, [2001] 1 S.C.R. 772 [hereinafter *Trinity*].

14 Ibid.

15 *Chamberlain* v. *Surrey School District No. 36*, [2002] 4 S.C.R. 710.

16 *Trinity*, supra note 13.

17 *Smitherman* v. *Powers* (2002), 59 O.R. (3d) 423.

18 *Brillinger* v. *Brockie*, [2002] O.J. No. 2375.

19 *Owens* v. *Saskatchewan (Human Rights Commission)*, [2002] S.J. No. 732.

20 *Kempling* v. *British Columbia College of Teachers*, 2004 BCSC 133.

21 "Court Lifts Ban on Gay Marriages," *National Post*, 13 July 2002, p. A6. Cf. the warning comment in Rabbi Novak's *Halpern* affidavit (supra note 11 at 8): "Furthermore, if same-sex civil unions are recognized as a marital right in Canada, then those many religious communities that refuse to recognize them as such, much less solemnize them, could easily be identified as discriminatory according to civil law."

22 *House of Commons Debates Official Report* (Hansard), 8 June 1999 at 15967–8.

23 C-250 received royal assent on 29 Apr. 2004. As the official summary states, "This enactment expands the definition 'identifiable group' relating to the area of hate propaganda in the Criminal Code to include any section of the public distinguished by sexual orientation." The bill does include an exemption, "if, in good faith, the person expressed or attempted to establish by an argument an opinion on a religious subject or an opinion based on a belief in a religious text."

24 In both *R. v. Keegstra* [1990] 3 S.C.R. 697 and *R. v. Harding* (2001), 57 O.R. (3d) 333, Christians tried to use this defence. The court's interpretation boils down to this: if we consider it to be promoting hatred, it cannot qualify as a "good faith" opinion on a religious subject. This circular reasoning removes this as an effective defence.

25 EFC Oral Submission on Bill C-250, 13 May 2003, p. 4.

THREE

The Excuses

RIGHTS AND RECOGNITION

Rights and Recognition

Douglas Farrow

The reason given over and over again in the Canadian debate for changing the definition of marriage – or, to be more accurate, for attempting to replace marriage with a different institution, whether of the same name or some other – is that marriage is an institution that violates the equality rights of homosexuals. It is precisely as an equality-rights issue that the proposed change provides cover for politicians who wish to embrace it, or feel compelled to embrace it. And it is precisely as an equality-rights issue that it is least understood and least defensible. No other country in the world has made the claim that Canada appears set to make: that marriage as we have known it constitutes a rights violation. The United Nations Human Rights Commission has, in practice, denied that it does.[1] If only out of a sense of responsibility to promote a valid international human-rights discourse – though there are many other good reasons – we must pause to reconsider this matter.

The equality-rights case goes something like this: Marriage is a close personal relationship between two consenting adults, involving sexual intimacy and a long-term commitment, which is formalized by public vows and public recognition. The additional assumption or stipulation traditionally made, that the two adults in question will be of different sexes, excludes homosexuals and denies to same-sex unions the public legitimacy of heterosexual unions. In so doing, it demeans homosexual persons and affronts their dignity, by implying that their capacity to love is deficient or that their love is somehow unworthy of public approval. Adding injury to insult, it also denies them the full range of privileges of married heterosexuals. For these reasons, it must be denounced as a rights violation and disallowed, as in fact it has been, under the equality-rights section (section 15) of the *Canadian Charter of Rights and Freedoms*. Parliament must follow the courts in this matter, not merely out of a principled refusal to use section 33, which allows federal and provincial legislatures to declare a law valid notwithstanding certain *Charter* provisions,[2] but because the courts are morally as well as legally right in the decision they have reached. Marriage must be redefined as a union of two persons without consideration of gender, so as to become properly inclusive of all Canadians.[3]

Now in passing it is worth pointing out, to those who wish to be principled supporters of the *Charter*, that section 33 is as much a part of the *Charter* as is any other section. If section 33 can with impunity be rejected in principle, then so can any other section or provision. The notion that the *Charter* can be protected elsewhere only by repudiating it here is an odd one, to say the least. However, my purpose is to rebut the rights argument, not defend section 33. My rebuttal will proceed in four stages. In so far as it is persuasive, the question of invoking section 33 may need to be revisited.

1. The equality-rights argument is viciously circular

To proceed at all, we need to notice that the main rights argument amounts to a nice piece of subterfuge. Its conclusion is that marriage must be redefined. This distracts us from the fact that marriage has *already* been redefined in the argument's very first move. That is, a new category – the "close personal adult relationship" – has been invented to provide a framework for our understanding of marriage.[4] Once this framework is accepted, it follows that homosexual unions can be marriage-like and, in that case, should qualify as marriage. If marriage is nothing but a certain form of publicly acknowledged sexual intimacy and commitment between two persons, one to which gender and biology and procreation are not directly relevant, why should the two persons not be of the same sex? Would we not be discriminating against such persons by denying to their relationship the name and benefits of marriage? And what requires such a denial? Merely the common-law definition of marriage as the union of a man and woman. So let us change the definition and write into law that marriage is a close personal relationship between adults, a union of two persons. That will erase the discrimination and resolve the equality-rights violation. Marriage will be open to homosexuals.

This argument is obviously circular, and viciously so. Certainly there can be nothing wrong with saying that, if marriage is simply a union of two persons, two persons of the same sex must not be denied a marriage licence. Nor is it necessarily wrong (though it may be foolish) to write into law that marriage is, or rather will be, simply a union of two persons. It is wrong, however, to claim that we *must* write this new definition into law in order to avoid unconstitutional discrimination and equality-rights violations, when in fact no such discrimination or violation is possible until after the new definition is in place.[5]

Let me explain. One of the necessary conditions for a violation of equality rights is differential treatment that cannot be rationally justified. Exclusion of homosexuals from marriage would appear to be a bald form of differential treatment, whether or not rationally justified. But the traditional definition of marriage makes no such exclusion. Since marriage is between a male and a female, and all people are either male or female, marriage is in principle open to all people. The fact that for a wide variety of reasons – of which homosexuality is but one – not all people are cut out for marriage changes nothing. As Richard Posner, Chief Judge, United States Court of Appeals for the Seventh Circuit, points out, "in this respect there is already perfect formal equality between homosexuals and heterosexuals."[6]

The new definition does not produce a broader institution. Instead it produces an institution with sub-categories that are not universally inclusive.

What happens when we say, instead, that marriage is simply a union of two persons? Do we broaden marriage or make it more inclusive? What is already universal cannot be made more universal. The new definition does not produce a broader institution. Instead it produces an institution with sub-categories that are *not* universally inclusive (male "marriages" and female "marriages"). This raises the spectre of exclusion, since in principle it becomes possible to permit only men to marry, or only women. But not only is this spectre rather pathetic, frightening no one; on the traditional definition it cannot even be conjured up! Yet it is the traditional definition that same-sex marriage advocates falsely say is haunted by it.[7]

Let us consider a more subtle form of differential treatment, however. Heterosexuals, it is claimed, are free to marry the person of their choice (assuming, of course, that the choice is mutual) while homosexuals are not. So there is differential treatment after all, and what looks like an equality-rights violation. But that is just more hocus-pocus, another illusion created by the circularity of the argument. The freedom to marry the person of one's choice is still a freedom to marry. And what does "marry" mean? That, of course, is what is at issue. If marriage is the union of a man and a woman, the freedom to marry the person of one's choice cannot mean the freedom of a man to marry a man; so denying a marriage licence to two men cannot be an infringement of that freedom. Only after the definition of marriage has already been altered by judicial fiat to "a union of two persons" is such an infringement possible.

When we have noticed this, we will also see that we are not reduced to claiming that it is reasonable, in the sense allowed by section 1 of the *Charter*,[8] to restrict the right of homosexuals to marry. In other words, we are not forced to say that there is differential treatment of homosexuals, but that this differential treatment is justified by some higher good. There is certainly a place for that kind of argument, as we will later discover, but that place is not here. On the contrary, we are insisting here on the right – or rather, the freedom – of homosexuals to marry, while denying their right to demand the redefinition of marriage on equality-rights grounds.[9]

Before we leave this section, let me clear up one possible misunderstanding. I have been charging some same-sex marriage advocates (and their supporters on our judicial benches) with employing a viciously circular argument. I say "some" because I am only speaking of those who actually use such an argument. It is perfectly possible to be an advocate of same-sex marriage without doing so. The only problem is that one cannot then appeal to equality rights, at least not in this way, with a view to changing the definition by force of law. Instead one would have to find some other way to invoke equality rights – we are about to come to that – or else try to persuade the public that redefining marriage is the right thing to do on other grounds altogether.

2. The equality-rights argument invokes a false understanding of human dignity

So much for the first stage of our rebuttal. The second stage is more difficult – not intellectually but on the ground – because it requires us to challenge one of the fundamentals of *Charter* jurisprudence as we presently know it, namely, the notion that human dignity, in Justice Iacobucci's words, "means that an individual or group feels self-respect and self-worth."[10] Those in favour of redefinition have leaned heavily on this notion, and indeed it is one on which they must depend all the more as the logical flaw at the foundations of the equality-rights argument is exposed.

Obviously we are dealing once again with a question of definition – in this case the definition of dignity – but here at least there is no subterfuge, so long as it is not claimed that the Iacobucci definition is itself constitutional. For there is nothing constitutional about it. It is merely an interpretive instrument that, more or less arbitrarily, has been brought by the courts to bear on the Constitution. That said, it is really quite astonishing that this concept of human dignity should gain such a high level of currency, given its intrinsic poverty of meaning and impracticality under law (not to speak of education or psychology). If my human dignity rests on whether or not I feel self-respect, then it may well go up and down like a yo-yo. It may show itself to be subject to no canons of reason but only to the changing and unreliable measure of this or that personal or corporate ambition. Moreover, it is most likely to function competitively, pitting me or my identity group over against some other person or group.

If my human dignity rests on whether or not I feel self-respect, then it may well go up and down like a yo-yo.

The latter problem – of zero-sum competition – is serious enough for the same-sex marriage debate, and can be illustrated by the Chrétien government's *Proposal for an Act respecting certain aspects of legal capacity for marriage for civil purposes* (2003). The preamble to this draft legislation indicates that redefining marriage to make it accessible to same-sex couples will "reflect values of tolerance, respect and equality" consistent with the *Charter*. But of course it follows that those who oppose redefinition do not reflect such values. This charge, publicly made and enshrined in law, can only diminish the respect in which such people are held, and may in turn diminish their own sense of dignity. In other words, there are winners and losers here, though there are not supposed to be: the need to affirm one person's or one group's dignity requires us to call into question another's. The dignity question thus becomes a game of power, of struggle for control. Words like "tolerance" or "respect" become pawns in this game; to win it one must wield them with strategic (not to say Machiavellian) foresight. Our courts have not yet fully reckoned with this problem, though most of our law schools have grasped it well enough and for obvious reasons have set themselves the task of teaching the game to their students.

The former problem – subjectivity – is still more serious, however, because more fundamental. It was partly acknowledged already in *Law v. Canada*, where Justice Iacobucci qualified the court's concern with the subjective side of human dignity: Any inquiry into how "a person legitimately feels when confronted with a particular law" must be conducted from no other perspective than that of the claimant. (In the Bible, and *Law* is fast becoming a kind of bible, one would expect to see a *selah* at this point, indicating a pause for sober reflection.) Yet "a court must be satisfied that the claimant's assertion that differential treatment imposed by legislation demeans his or her dignity is supported by an objective assessment of the situation."[11] The addition of an objective criterion is meant to protect us from the chaos of the purely arbitrary. Unfortunately, once we take the subjective as our starting point – and this is what is new and distinctive about *Charter* jurisprudence as moulded by the instrument in question[12] – we are stuck with its implications. If human dignity is at bottom a matter of how I feel about myself, then I myself become both the measure and the measurer of human dignity. This is incompatible with the very concept of the rule of law, which requires a starting point in something that is the same for

> If human dignity is at bottom a matter of how I feel about myself, then I myself become both the measure and the measurer of human dignity. This is incompatible with the very concept of the rule of law.

all. Allied to so alien a principle, the law can only become a vehicle of confusion and oppression rather than of clarity and liberation.[13]

In other words, the concept of human dignity now at play in Canadian jurisprudence is incurably subjectivist. It needs to be ditched in favour of something more properly objective before it and *Charter* law become altogether dysfunctional. Take, by way of contrast, the concept of human dignity that rests on a doctrine of the imago dei or image of God. Such a concept (be it Jewish, Christian, Muslim, Kantian, etc.) is capable of distinguishing between one's human worth and one's feelings. However one feels about oneself, however others feel about one, one's basic human dignity is upheld by God, who is himself its inviolable guarantor. This allows a reasonable distinction between act and agent, or between sin and sinner, to use the traditional language. It liberates both the individual and society from the need to respond to every vacillation in public or private sentiment. It permits stability in law, allowing it to resist erosion by the tides of public opinion. That is one reason, surely, why the *Charter*'s preamble links recognition of the rule of law to recognition of the supremacy of God.[14]

All of this is jeopardized by the new subjectivist notion of human dignity, and by the insatiable appetite for public recognition and approval that is its inevitable byproduct. The subjectivist approach requires constant public reassurance, since it is inherently unstable. Those who adopt it are never content, nor can they be. But the attempt to satisfy their voracious appetites, sure to be diverse and conflicting, can only pull society apart and bring the law itself into disrepute. For public acceptance cannot be legislated, nor in any case can legislation hope to keep up with the shifting tides. The undertow of this or that hasty decision – such as the removal of procreation from the concept of marriage, a point to which we will return – will carry the lawmakers too far from shore for them to keep their feet when the next wave breaks.

But to the immediate argument. There are, as I said, those who acknowledge the circularity we criticized in phase one of this rebuttal. They still claim, however, that there is an equality-rights violation that mandates the redefinition of marriage. This violation becomes visible and palpable in the pain experienced by homosexuals when their own preferred form of union is not honoured with the honour reserved for marriage. (To make the pain itself visible and palpable, of course, is the task of their advocates in the court and in the press.) That society should have an institution such as marriage, which honours certain heterosexual unions while failing to honour certain homosexual unions that are at least partly analogous, is ipso facto to inflict pain on participants in the latter through differential treatment that cannot be rationally justified. This differential treatment does not so much restrict their freedom as impugn their dignity. It must have as its remedy a means of alleviating their feeling of injury and restoring their pride or self-respect – the obvious, though not necessarily the only, means for doing so being the loosening of the definition of marriage to accommodate their unions.

Now I am not convinced that this argument can be strictly separated from the circularity of its companion argument, a matter that might be probed by inquiring into a fallacy of equivocation respecting the word "union." But that is not what I want to do here. Rather, I want to apply the general critique just developed. That some homosexuals feel demeaned because they are denied not marriage – for marry they may if they choose – but the power to call same-sex partnerships "marriage," does not mean that their dignity has been undermined. It does not mean that their section 15 equality rights have been violated. It means only that they have a certain perception, whether true or false, about what those who hold the traditional view of marriage think about them. And this – what is actually thought and what is thought to be thought – should not matter under the law at a foundational level. It is neither uniform nor ascertainable with any degree of certainty.[15] Nor does it go anywhere near the heart of human dignity or of human rights. Human dignity does not depend on mere opinion, whether my own or someone else's. As for rights, everyone has a right to self-defence in the face of some direct and particular attack on their reputation, but no one has a right to be thought well of, much less to be assured that they are thought well of.

No one has a right to be thought well of, much less to be assured that they are thought well of.

But who, you might well respond, is arguing in a circle now? Farrow doesn't like the Iacobucci definition of dignity, which leads to different conclusions about the necessity of redefining marriage than does his own definition. Unfortunately for Farrow, it is the Iacobucci definition that is operative in the law. And it was already operative before *Halpern* v. *Canada*[16] and other same-sex marriage judgments. So the judgments that rest on it are, to that extent, sound; their reasoning is circular, to be sure, but not viciously circular. All this, I think, must be admitted, which brings me back to my point about constitutionality. The Iacobucci, or *Law*, definition does not belong to the Constitution; it is subject to review and reconsideration in a way that the Constitution is not.

My objection to the Iacobucci definition is occasioned by, but not rooted in, my objection to same-sex marriage. I say this not only to protect myself from a charge of begging the question, but also to underline the fact that what is at stake in the great Canadian marriage debate goes even deeper than the question of marriage itself. That marriage is fundamental to human sociality in this world of ours, I do not doubt. That it is therefore a subject worthy of full-blown political debate, and that this debate must become a defining moment for our society, I do not question. Some today are talking not only about invoking the notwithstanding clause but about a constitutional amendment to preserve the traditional definition of marriage. For reasons that will become clearer in the final section of this essay, I support such talk. But I wonder whether we might do better to write into the Constitution, not that marriage means the union of a man and a woman, but that dignity means something other and more than that a person or group feels self-respect. For dignity on that definition is neither inviolable nor reliable. It is not a basis for law but a recipe for social turmoil.

I am, of course, only half serious about this suggestion. As David Feldman, Dean of the Faculty of Law in the University of Birmingham, has written: "Human dignity is already an important background value for human-rights law and constitutional development in international law and in a growing number of national jurisdictions . . . On the other hand, dignity has been revealed . . . to be a highly complex concept. The content of its central core is not clear, making it an uncertain guide."[17] Doubtless we are not ready for a constitutional definition of dignity, then. But neither are we ready to concede the Iacobucci definition and allow it to be used by the courts to short-circuit the public debate about same-sex marriage.

Our lack of clarity respecting the concept of human dignity stems from two sources, according to Feldman. One is the fact that the term operates with a variety of referents and in a variety of ways.[18] The other is "a lack of agreement about what makes human life good, both for individuals and for societies." The third stage of my rebuttal of the rights argument requires me to venture much further into this latter realm, taking up a number of tasks at once. I will begin with the easiest, which is to point out that the main goal of the equality-rights argument is not the defence of homosexuals but the celebration of homosexuality. Afterward I will try to assess the significance of that fact by touching briefly on several controversial points.

3. The equality-rights argument is an inapposite defence of homosexuality

In *Goodridge* v. *Massachusetts*, Justice Greaney (concurring with the majority) opines that "simple principles of decency" make it right to extend "full acceptance, tolerance and respect" to same-sex couples by identifying their unions as marriages. "Because marriage is, by all accounts, the cornerstone of our social structure, as well as the defining relationship in our personal lives, confining eligibility in the institution, and all of its accompanying benefits and responsibilities, to opposite-sex couples is basely unfair."[19] Quoting *Griswold* v. *Connecticut*, he insists that same-sex couples also come together in an association that is "intimate to the degree of being sacred," promoting "a way of life, not causes; a harmony in living, not political faiths; a bilateral loyalty, not commercial or social projects."[20] To refuse them marriage would be ignoble as well as unreasonable.[21]

The minority judges did not challenge their colleagues' high evaluation of marriage as a social good. They did, however, challenge the notion that same-sex marriage suits are simply about access to an established way of life and not about a cause or the promotion of a political faith. Justice Cordy, while praising "the courageous efforts of many [that] have resulted in increased dignity, rights, and respect for gay and lesbian members of our community," is quite frank: "This case is not about government intrusions into matters of personal liberty. It is not about the rights of same-sex couples to live together, to be intimate with each other, or to adopt and raise children together. It is about whether the State must endorse and support their choices by changing the institution of civil marriage to make its benefits, obligations, and responsibilities applicable to them."[22] That the state *might* so endorse and support, he concludes, is reasonably contemplated; that the state *must* so endorse is judicial infringement on legislative freedom.

Outside the courtroom, few will deny that endorsement is the goal. And the endorsement sought is not merely for the principle of individual choice. No, it is endorsement of a group, defined by its characteristics and culture; as such it is also endorsement of a lifestyle and a particular set of choices. Bruce MacDougall, a legal advocate for same-sex marriage, offers an analysis in which he traces a movement from the condemnation to the celebration of these choices:

> The field of discourse about legal equality can be divided into three main sites away from the beginning site of condemnation: compassion, condonation, and celebration. To have full legal equality within a society, members of a (minority) group need: 1) to be free from discrimination (compassion); 2) to have access to benefits others have (condonation); and 3) to be included as a valuable group by the society (celebration). That debate in Canada with respect to gay and lesbian rights has moved to symbolic issues such as pride day proclamations, content in school curricula, and marriage, means discussion is now at the site of celebration. Success on these matters would represent state, which is legal, acceptance and celebration of the group. It would represent state approval of a group in a positive, active and symbolic way that other state actions such as non-discrimination protection and conferral of benefits do in a non-public or less public and more individualized way.[23]

Two things immediately require to be said. First, those of MacDougall's persuasion might well reject my way of putting the matter when I say that the goal of the equality-rights argument is not the defence of homosexuals but the celebration of homosexuality and the "gay" lifestyle. In their minds this is one and the same thing. Human identity, sexual orientation, sexual acts, and the culture that surrounds and supports these acts are seamlessly interwoven. To defend that culture is all of a piece with defending homosexuals. One cannot defend homosexuals merely as individual human persons, for that is not to defend them at all. It is to leave them open to that most despised instrument of a past religious culture, the distinction between the sinner and his sin.[24]

It is not possible to pursue here the profound questions that must be asked and answered before this disagreement can even be measured, let alone resolved. But we do not need to. For the second thing to be said is that neither cultures nor lifestyles have rights. Persons have rights, and groups may have rights, but cultures and lifestyles do not. The equality-rights argument, then, has to be mounted in defence of persons or of groups, not of cultures or lifestyles, if it is going to be mounted at all. To be sure, there is still a very large gray area here. Group rights is notoriously difficult terrain for law and public policy, into which the marriage issue has introduced perplexing new obstacles. Even in the hands of learned judges it is frequently unclear, for example, whether the rights in question are those of specific persons, of certain couples qua couples, or of homosexuals generally.[25] What is clear enough, however, is that the label "marriage" has become a prize to be fought for, and that the legal battles over it – though they cannot be framed in terms of the approval of homosexual modes of life as such, but must rather be framed in terms of the right of homosexuals to adopt and to benefit from the "couple-centred" way of life normally associated with heterosexuals – are really about approval. Each victory is victory for a cause: complete public acceptance of homosexuality and of homosexual modes of life, however atypical of those modes "gay marriage" may be.[26] And from the standpoint of equality rights this is simply wrong. An equality-rights argument is an inapposite defence of homosexuality, if by homosexuality we mean anything more than mere sexual orientation.

It is widely supposed that all of this can be safely ignored if the problem of homosexuality can be made analogous to that of race or of gender. But it isn't. Homosexuality is not biologically based in the way that race is.[27] It is not an inherited set of physical attributes largely irrelevant to social function. It is a much more complex phenomenon, a social and psychological phenomenon that in the last analysis is

> *N*either cultures nor lifestyles have rights. Persons have rights, and groups may have rights, but cultures and lifestyles do not.

about ways of feeling, thinking, and acting. In so far as there are rights questions involved here, then, they are not susceptible to the same analysis as rights protecting racial minorities, which are supposed to keep the irrelevant – biology not behaviour – irrelevant.[28] We get closer to something analogous when we turn to gender; for gender, too, though it has obvious biological determinants, is a highly complex matter. If it were not, the issue of homosexuality would not arise. But here again the analogy does not work. Homosexuality is not something *like* gender; it is not comparable with being male or female. Rather it is about experiencing and handling gender in unusual ways. Again, it is about behaviour rather than about biology. That is why it is relevant rather than irrelevant, and why it is not properly understood as a matter of equality rights.[29]

The equality-rights argument depends on these bogus analogies for cover. With their loss goes the last excuse for refusing to recognize that societies, like individuals, are also free to choose – or rather, are compelled to choose – which behaviours and modes of life they wish to honour or invest in, and which they do not. Such choices are sometimes moral and sometimes merely prudential, but they must be made and their consequences borne. No equality-rights argument can relieve us of the choice in the present instance; nor can it justify the choice that we make. Is homosexuality among the former? Is it something in which we think we should invest? If so, in which of its various possible expressions?

The reader who fears that I am about to launch an attack on this or that homosexual mode of life can relax. I am merely trying to establish the fact that the high ground of equality rights does not belong to those who advocate same-sex marriage. It does not belong to anyone where same-sex marriage is concerned. We are free to debate whether or not supporting homosexuality, in this way or some other, is an appropriate use of our collective resources. In order to reach an answer, however, we will indeed have to make some determination respecting the goodness and the social utility of homosexual modes of life. One of the curiously self-contradictory features of the marriage debate is that it is being conducted as if our society were under some moral obligation not to

The high ground of equality rights does not belong to those who advocate same-sex marriage.

do that. How very odd, when the social revolution we are currently experiencing *is* a revolution in moral obligation and moral judgment, with the celebration of same-sex marriage serving as its public sacrament. But here is another contradictory feature: if we embrace that sacrament, are we not passing judgment on those in the homosexual community (the vast majority, by most accounts) who prefer what used to be called a promiscuous lifestyle? The solution to this second contradiction, of course, is either no marriages or open marriages, options some are already advancing.[30] Their mention, however, brings us to the final stage of my rebuttal.

4. The equality-rights argument can succeed only by betraying children

Society's support for marriage is already both a moral and a prudential judgment, whether or not same-sex marriage comes into view. That judgment is not – this we may happily concede! – about either heterosexuality or homosexuality per se, but about a particular nexus of human bonds and their supporting domestic relations. Society is not bound to treat all such bonds or relations equally. It is not bound to say, for example, that one form of cohabitation is no better than another, or that all households with children will be regarded alike.[31] And if society can and should regard all *persons* as equal, it should not and cannot regard all social or all sexual activity (even if consensual) as equal. That is why it endorses an institution such as marriage in the first place. Marriage is not only endorsed, but honoured and rewarded, because it cultivates certain of the necessary conditions for human flourishing.

A few of these must be noted here. Traditionally in our society, the roots of which were nourished in Christendom, the primary goods of marriage have been three: bonding or union (sacramentum), chastity or faithfulness (fides), and procreation (proles).[32] In the common-law definition of marriage, the first shows up as "the voluntary union for life of one man and one woman" and the second as "to the exclusion of all others"; the third appears only implicitly, in the stipulation "one man and one woman." Now each of these was regarded as implying the others. Even in its civil dimensions, marriage was viewed as a threefold cord, the strength of which lay in the intertwining of these goods. Marriage as bonding or union helped, among other things, to address one of the obvious difficulties facing every society: the bridging of the sex divide. Marriage as an exclusive commitment helped, on the one hand, to minimize (though it could not eliminate) the commodification of women and children, and on the other hand to facilitate (though it could not guarantee) the orderly transfer of material goods.[33] Marriage as the approved context for procreation served society's interest in reproducing itself through the cultivation of bonds of loyalty between the generations. It served to bring the interests of parents and the interests of the state into harmony where the production and nurture of children are concerned.

Chief among these intertwining goods, at least from the civil point of view, has been the third. As Justice Cordy writes, "It is difficult to imagine a State purpose more important and legitimate than ensuring, promoting, and supporting an optimal social structure within which to bear and raise children."[34] But herewith the problem. The new definition of marriage imposed by the courts, since it makes heterosexuality optional rather than axiomatic, disconnects marriage from procreation. It cuts the primary strand, allowing the entire cord to unravel and eventually to snap.[35] That is no accident, but a necessary byproduct of the equal-rights argument. It is something that simply must be done, because the good of procreation is the good most obviously not transferable to same-sex partnerships.

Our current low birth rate and apparent antipathy to children are the antecedent conditions that expose this strand to the knife. That the knife itself is a blunt instrument, and clumsily wielded, has been noticed; which is to say, it has been observed by many that the new definition is vague to the point of being unsustainable in public policy.[36] What has been too little noticed, however – or, more precisely, what has been deliberately hidden, to our collective shame – is the obvious fact that it is, indeed, wielded against children.[37] For to redefine marriage in such a way as to disconnect it from procreation is necessarily to dismantle the only institution we have that honours a child's natural right (recognized in the *United Nations Convention on the Rights of the Child*) "to know and be cared for by his or her parents."[38] That right, of course, is a prima facie one; it represents an ideal that cannot always be maintained in practice. But to sever the link between procreation and marriage is to abandon even the ideal. It is to withdraw from children the formal commitment of society to the fact that their place, as far as may be possible, is with their own father and mother. The damage this must eventually do to the sanctity of the parent–child bond, in the name of a spurious equality right for homosexuals, is incalculable. So is the damage it will do to our society generally. Now, not later, is the time for us to ask: If marriage ceases to dignify the bond between father, mother, and child – the bond wherein we learn and practise the basic virtues of loyalty and commitment – what *will* it dignify?[39]

It is at this point that the circular argument we have criticized becomes vicious in a second sense. As discussed, it becomes *logically* vicious when it calls for the imposition of a new definition of marriage in order to eradicate a form of discrimination that only comes into existence with that definition. But it also becomes *practically* vicious in so far as it succeeds in divorcing procreation from marriage, and so in prying children out from under the protective umbrella of an institution designed to hold together the offspring of sexual union with their natural mothers and fathers.[40] That this is justified, as it often is, in the name of support for the children of parents who have taken them out of marriages into same-sex partnerships, is not surprising in our divorce culture. But, considered on its own merits, it is nonetheless explicable only as an act of determined cynicism. Can we see it otherwise, when we are asked to sacrifice the very principle of the parent–child bond, which only an opposite-sex institution can secure, on the altar of redefinition?

Conclusion

Some time ago I wrote in one of our national newspapers that the debate we are having about marriage "is a debate about what marriage is, or what we would like it to become, which has been disguised as a human rights debate so as to provide leverage in the courts."[41] Some of our courts have welcomed this disguise, and deployed the equality-rights argument to foreclose on the debate. In doing so they have violated the principle of the right chooser, and this violation has thrown Canada into a double crisis. As a society we must now make two decisions rather than one. We must decide whether permitting the judiciary to act in this way is consistent with a limited constitutional democracy, and we must decide the definition itself.

Regarding the former, I will remark only that the question of process is already a matter of sufficient gravity to warrant the use, if necessary, of section 33, the *Charter*'s provision for a time of crisis. It is not for judges to tell us what marriage is, or rather what it must become.[42] Regarding the latter, which is the question of substance, I must say a bit more by way of conclusion. For we are asking here, in

We must decide whether permitting the judiciary to act in this way is consistent with a limited constitutional democracy, and we must decide the definition itself.

our way, after the very foundations of civil society. What will lie at those foundations in the place reserved for the rock called "marriage"? A commitment to honouring sexually intimate couples, or a commitment to honouring the network of bonds that begins with husband and wife and extends (under normal circumstances) to father, mother, and children?

If we opt for honouring couples, we do not altogether exclude in practice, but we do exclude in principle, support for the richer nexus of human bonding at which marriage has always aimed. As a civil institution, marriage will no longer be able to lend formal support to that nexus; its support will be incidental rather than axiomatic. If, on the other hand, we choose to maintain the tradition, we must accept the fact that marriage offers no institutional support to a particular kind of couple, the homosexual couple. That is the moment of truth behind the equality-rights argument for changing the definition of marriage. Are we left, then, on the horns of a dilemma?

If we are, it is not the equality-rights argument that puts us there, for we have seen that it is fatally flawed. The equality-rights argument is viciously circular, requiring redefinition in order to justify redefinition. It demands assent to a largely untested and highly deficient notion of human dignity. It passes illegitimately from the equality of persons to a putative equality of lifestyles, in the hope of effecting a judicially enforced moral reassessment of a particular set of lifestyles; that is, it abuses human-rights discourse to attain the goal of the public celebration of homosexuality. Last but not least, the redefinition it requires eviscerates marriage of its foremost public purpose, by detaching it from procreation and revoking its formal commitment to the welfare of children.

But does the possibility of a dilemma remain, at least for those who believe that institutional support for homosexual couples (qua couples) is a good and worthy objective? I see no reason to think so. That marriage, if it is to continue to serve the socially crucial nexus generated by procreation, cannot offer *its* support does not mean that no institutional support is conceivable. The failure of the equality-rights argument, however, means that other proposals for support (civil unions, for example) will have to be sold to the public on their own merits, if any. That is as it should be. For public recognition of particular life choices is not a matter of rights.

Notes

1 In 2002 the United Nations Human Rights Commission refused to hear a complaint against the New Zealand Court of Appeal when the latter denied (in *Quilter v. New Zealand (A.G.)* [1997] ICHRL 129) that the prohibition against discrimination on grounds of sexual orientation implied a right to same-sex marriage. The attempt to establish such a right has first met with some success in Canada, though Canada's *Charter*, unlike New Zealand's *Bill of Rights*, does not mention sexual orientation.

2 Section 33 (1) reads as follows: "Parliament or the legislature of a province may expressly declare in an Act of Parliament or of the legislature, as the case may be, that the Act or a provision thereof shall operate notwithstanding a provision included in section 2 or sections 7 to 15 of this *Charter*." This renewable declaration is effective for five years.

3 Thus also, in America, the majority decision in *Goodridge v. Massachusetts* No. 08860 (Mass. S.J.C. 2003) [hereinafter *Goodridge*], which leans on *Halpern v. Canada* (2003), O.A.C. 172 [hereinafter *Halpern*].

4 See *Beyond Conjugality: Recognizing and Supporting Close Personal Adult Relationships*, Law Commission of Canada, 2001.

5 Justice Cordy, one of the three dissenters in *Goodridge* (supra note 3), observes this circularity: "Only by assuming that 'marriage' includes the union of two persons of the same sex does the court conclude that restricting marriage to opposite-sex couples infringes on the 'right' of same-sex couples to 'marry.'" And he adds (n. 46): "The same semantic sleight of hand could transform every other restriction on marriage into an infringement of a right of fundamental importance."

6 R.A. Posner, reviewing William Eskridge's *The Case for Same-Sex Marriage* (New York: Free Press, 1996): "Should There Be Homosexual Marriage? And If So, Who Should Decide?" *Michigan Law Review* 95 (1996–1997): 1580.

7 Sometimes the more modest argument is made – shifting from the logic of marriage to its arithmetic – that permitting same-sex marriage will at least encourage a greater number of actual marriages. But this, too, is fallacious. One cannot make more of one thing simply by declaring another thing to be the same thing.

8 Section 1 of the *Charter* "guarantees the rights and freedoms set out in it subject only to such reasonable limits prescribed by law as can be demonstrably justified in a free and democratic society."

9 That is something Justice Blair of the Ontario Superior Court (*Halpern* v. *Canada*, [2002] O.J. No. 2714 at para. 99ff [hereinafter *Halpern* (2002)]) seems not to grasp. He begins to wrestle with the problem of circularity, and goes on to argue that within the logic of the traditional definition, same-sex couples are not excluded from marriage "on the basis of a personal characteristic giving rise to differential treatment founded upon a stereotypical difference," hence no section 15 violation of that kind occurs. Then he adds: "Same-sex couples are [on this view] simply incapable of marriage because they cannot procreate through heterosexual intercourse. Thus it is a distinction created by the nature of the institution itself which precludes homosexuals from access to marriage." But this is not right. Same-sex couples may be incapable of marriage but homosexuals are not. Homosexuals do have access to marriage as traditionally defined, and are not excluded.

10 This is the definition to which *Halpern* (2002), (ibid. at introduction, para. 3) appeals: "In *Law* v. *Canada (Minister of Employment and Immigration)*, [1999] 1 S.C.R. 497 at 530, Iacobucci J., writing for a unanimous court, described the importance of human dignity: 'Human dignity means that an individual or group feels self-respect and self-worth. It is concerned with physical and psychological integrity and empowerment. Human dignity is harmed by unfair treatment premised upon personal traits or circumstances which do not relate to individual needs, capacities, or merits. It is enhanced by laws which are sensitive to the needs, capacities, and merits of different individuals, taking into account the context underlying their differences. Human dignity is harmed when individuals and groups are marginalized, ignored, or devalued, and is enhanced when laws recognize the full place of all individuals and groups within Canadian society.'"

11 *Law* v. *Canada (Minister of Employment and Immigration)*, [1999] 1 S.C.R. 497 at 530 at para. 60 [hereinafter Law].

12 See *Law*, para. 3.

13 Picking up the quotation from para. 53, where *Halpern* (supra note 9) leaves off: "Human dignity within the meaning of the equality guarantee does not relate to the status or position of an individual in society *per se*, but rather concerns the manner in which a person legitimately feels when confronted with a particular law. Does the law treat him or her unfairly, taking into account all of the circumstances regarding the individuals affected and excluded by the law?" Here is the recipe for endless legal interventions and counter-interventions in the lives of ordinary Canadians. Para. 54 goes on to insist that the "overriding concern with protecting and promoting human dignity in the sense just described

infuses all elements of the discrimination analysis" as determined by section 15(1) of the *Charter*.

14 On the preamble, cf. my "Of Secularity and Civil Religion" in D. Farrow, ed., *Recognizing Religion in a Secular Society*, chap. 9 (Montreal: McGill-Queen's University Press, 2004); cf. also Jean Bethke Elshtain, "Persons, Politics, and a Catholic Understanding of Human Rights" (ibid., chap. 5).

15 Certainly it is highly susceptible to the manipulations of the spin doctors, as might be illustrated from the *Goodridge* case (supra note 3), e.g., which from the outset presents a false picture of the "gay family" as something statistically and socially analogous to what is normally meant by the word "family." This is necessary as a basis for establishing pain, unjustly inflicted by negative stereotyping, and the claim to redress for injured dignity.

16 *Halpern* (2002), supra note 9.

17 "Human Dignity as a Legal Value – Part II," *Public Law* (2000): 75. Part I is in *Public Law* (1999): 682–702.

18 This, for brevity's sake if not for clarity's, I have done my best to overlook.

19 *Goodridge*, supra note 3 at note 39. It may be asked, particularly by the unmarried, who exactly is the referent of "our."

20 *Griswold* v. *Connecticut* (381 U.S. 479 [1965] at 486) is the famous contraception case that established a new constitutional right to privacy. Note the phrase "intimate to the degree of being sacred," which begins the march toward the couple-centred view of marriage.

21 Justice Greaney differs from the rest of the majority, however, in arguing that what we have here is a gender-based "restriction of a fundamental right": Hillary should be free to marry whom she pleases. She pleases to marry Julie. She cannot do so because she (Hillary) is a woman. Ergo, her equality rights have been abridged on grounds of sex. One assumes that this curious contortion of logic, for which he offers a precedent in Vermont, was an embarrassment to the other three majority justices. In any case, it has nothing to do with "simple principles of decency."

22 *Goodridge*, supra note 3 at section D (Conclusion).

23 "The Celebration of Same-Sex Marriage" in *Ottawa Law Review* 32 (2001): 253, quoted by MacDougall in "A Respectful Distance: Appellate Courts Consider Religious Motivation of Public Figures in Homosexual Equality Discourse – The Cases of Chamberlain and Trinity Western University" in *U.B.C. Law Review* 35 (2002): 511–38.

24 MacDougall, interestingly, applies the act/agent distinction where religion is concerned while rejecting it in matters of sexuality. Presumably this reflects an anthropology that regards the human being as inherently or naturally sexual, but only accidentally or artificially religious. It is worth noting in defence of the religious alternative that the act/agent distinction, with which the sin/sinner distinction is bound up, serves as an instrument of mercy: one's sins may be rejected precisely because one's self is loved. But this requires a different sequence than MacDougall's. In place of condemnation, compassion, condonation, and celebration, it puts: compassion, condemnation, consolation (i.e., redemption), and celebration. In the choice between the one ordo salutis and the other lies the whole issue.

25 Both the language and the conceptual framework are slippery. Take, for example, the following remark by Justice Blair (*Halpern* (2002), supra note 9 at para. 103): "The evidence supports a conclusion that 'marriage' represents society's highest acceptance of the self-worth and the wholeness of a couple's relationship, and thus touches their sense of human dignity at its core." Does the couple have a unitary sense of dignity that may be the object of a rights violation? If so, are their rights being violated individually or as a couple? What are the implications of our answer to this question? (Of course, we are accepting here, for the sake of the argument, the mistaken notion that societal approval must touch the core of our sense of dignity. But must we make the additional mistake of supposing that the right to marry belongs to couples rather than to individuals?)

26 That is what has kept the anti-marriage faction of the "gay" community relatively quiet; but see, e.g., John McKellar, "The Irony of Same-Sex Marriage" in *Ethics & Medics* 27.12 (2002).

27 Homosexuality very likely has a biological component in some cases. But the popular and oft-repeated notion that it is biologically determined is nothing more than misinformation, based on the backwards reasoning that if homosexuality is like race it must be biologically based. The biological factors in homosexuality have continued to elude researchers, while evidence of the ability of some to change their sexual orientation has been growing (see, e.g., Robert Spitzer's recent study in the *Archives of Sexual Behavior* 32.5 [October 2003]: 403–17). More to the point is the ability of all to decide behaviour. On neither side of the debate should anyone wish to succumb to a robust determinism.

28 Were proof of a biological component for sexual orientation eventually to be provided, very little would follow in the way of rational conclusions about "gay rights," though the newspapers are full of articles assuming the latter and desperately seeking the former. Rights attach to persons not to genes – the rights of blacks, say, have precisely nothing to do with being black, everything to do with being human – and certainly not to inclinations or behaviours or modes of life. No one, we may hope, doubts that homosexuals are human persons.

29 Here I should comment further on the distinction between sexual orientation and homosexuality understood as a mode of life. The former is like race and gender in that it is not determinative of behaviour; the latter represents a set of behaviours. It is of course necessary to the "gay rights" or "gay marriage" cause to insist that no such distinction be drawn. But with that insistence the true nature of the cause is betrayed, together with its fundamental difference from the causes of racial minorities or women.

30 Attention to the rights of bisexuals, for example, would suggest the latter; attention to the rights of singles, the former. These putative rights, together with the legalization of polygamy and even of polyamory, are now being discussed in mainstream journals and newspapers.

31 "That the State does not preclude different types of families from raising children does not mean that it must view them all as equally optimal and equally deserving of State endorsement and support" (*Goodridge*, supra note 3 at section C.3, Justice Cordy).

32 These goods have social or civil dimensions as well as religious ones. Historically and hence religiously understood, they require a fuller and somewhat different presentation, for which see John Witte, Jr., *From Sacrament to Contract:*

Marriage, Religion, and Law in the Western Tradition (Louisville, KY: Westminster John Knox Press, 1997), pp. 218f.

33 The recognition of paternity was one important condition for that. Though we have other means for determining paternity today, the determination itself would be of little use in a society that no longer recognized the exclusive commitment of marriage.

34 See *Goodridge*, supra note 3 at section C.2, in which he points out that "the alternative, a society without the institution of marriage, in which heterosexual intercourse, procreation, and child care are largely disconnected processes, would be chaotic."

35 Sweden, which some years ago pioneered a marriage-like category for same-sex couples that it is only now getting round to calling "marriage," may stand as a witness to that process of unravelling, according to Stanley Kurtz (see "The End of Marriage in Scandinavia," *The Weekly Standard* 9.20, 2 Feb. 2004). Kurtz is quite right to point out, however, "that gay marriage is both an effect and a cause of the increasing separation between marriage and parenthood" (online edition, p. 2).

36 Exactly what sort of union does it have in view? Need it be sexual? Sexual or otherwise, why should it be a union of only two? Given that it is not necessarily or even normatively procreative, what marks this union out as something of particular value to society, worthy of public recognition and support?

37 Not, of course, in a literal sense – that we have already seen to in our abortion clinics, at a rate in Canada of over 100,000 per year. Given the country's bad conscience in that much more basic fact, its willingness to overlook the fact that it is now withdrawing in principle the support of marriage from birth children need not surprise us.

38 Note that this claim is evacuated of all meaning if the word "parents" is made to mean anything other than natural or biological parents. See also Professor Somerville's contribution above.

39 The answer, of course, is that it will dignify "the union for life of two persons" – that is, the love and commitment of couples. But once children are removed from the picture, the resultant "Valentine's Day" approach to the institution cannot sustain the "for life" ideal, any more than it can sustain the logic of two persons only. And then what?

40 Justice Cordy (*Goodridge*, supra note 3 at note 79) engages the *Goodridge* court on this point: "The court contends that the exclusive and permanent commitment of the marriage partnership rather than the begetting of children is the sine qua non of civil marriage, and that 'the "marriage is procreation" argument singles out the one unbridgeable difference between same-sex and opposite-sex couples, and transforms that difference into the essence of legal marriage.' The court has it backward. Civil marriage is the product of society's need to manage procreation as the inevitable consequence of intercourse between members of the opposite sex. Procreation has always been at the root of marriage and the reasons for its existence as a social institution. Its structure, one man and one woman committed for life, reflects society's judgment as how optimally to manage procreation and the resultant child-rearing. The court, in attempting to divorce procreation from marriage, transforms the form of the structure into its purpose. In doing so, it turns history on its head."

41 "The Marriage Debate Is Not a Human Rights Debate," *National Post*, 8 Oct. 2003.

42 The principle of the right chooser was acknowledged by Justice Blair in the original *Halpern* (2002) decision, (supra note 9) at para. 99: "I do not think," said he – though he voted with his colleagues – that "it is for the Court to choose between these various models of marriage, or for it to impose one form or another on society . . . ; these choices, in my view, are for legislators to make."

WHAT'S THE CHARTER GOT TO DO WITH IT?

What's the Charter Got to Do With It?

F.C. DeCoste

Like a person whose self-image is out of synch with how he really acts, the Canadian state gazes on itself proudly as liberal, freedom-granting, and justice-seeking, while its actions show it, in fact, to be post-liberal, enslaving, and unfair. This may be seen most clearly in the high-handed way it has taken a proprietorial interest in the institution of marriage and found it deficient according to its blueprint for the perfectly ordered society, the *Canadian Charter of Rights and Freedoms*.

But here's the question that must be asked: What's the *Charter* got to do with marriage? The purpose of this essay is to convince that the proper answer to this question is, "Nothing, nothing at all." By "proper answer," I mean the answer supplied by and grounded in the political morality that authorizes and limits the governance of a truly liberal-democratic state – the kind of state that Canada prides itself in being. And with just this answer, I mean as well to condemn as politically immoral the opposite view, presently ascendant in the executive and judicial branches of the Canadian state, that the institution of marriage – its meaning and its practice – is a proper object of state surveillance and supervision through the *Charter*.

The Canadian state's view proceeds from two premises that constitute its claim to sovereignty over marriage: (a) that marriage is a legal artefact and (b) that, as such, marriage must, at the election of any citizen – or, as it has happened, of any rights group – moved to raise the matter, conform to the constitutional standards proclaimed by the judicial branch of the Canadian state since 1982, when the *Charter* came into force. To discredit and, I hope, dishonour, these premises, I will do three things. First, I will show that, contra Canadian beliefs and practices, the notion of civil society is necessarily embedded in the liberal conception of political morality. Second, I will explore the relationship that must obtain between the state and the institutions and practices of civil society if the state is not to lose its liberal credentials and the authority of its law. Third, I will disclose the specifics of my charge of immorality against the recent conduct of the Canadian state regarding the institution and practice of marriage.

Political Morality and Civil Society

The liberal state – its law and its politics – is grounded on a distinction between personal matters and public matters. This is so because the liberal state is a limited state and because, absent such a distinction, there could be no means to chart the borders of state authority or, more precisely, to calculate the meaning of and the conduct required from an autonomy-respecting, because person-respecting, government. The state and its law are, consequently, expressions of a morality that is categorically different from the morality that properly governs personal and social life.

The object of personal morality is living a good life. The object of political morality is the good of political community. Because institutions are fundamental to a community's political life, it falls to political morality to tell us three things: what those institutions should be, "how [they] should be designed, [and] how people in them should act."[1] Concerning the first two matters, conceptions of political morality have minimally: (a) to identify the institutions required for a community's political life; (b) to structure the relations between those institutions; (c) to set standards for the treatment of members of political community by those institutions; and (d) to identify when those institutions may regulate relations between members of political community and in what fashion. The third matter concerns the institutional moralities that those institutions define for, and impose on, their officers.

The rule of law is, of course, the indisputable and indispensable core of the political morality of liberal states: all projects and purposes of the liberal state must both conform to its requirements and reside in its institutional architecture. The rule of law constitutes the legislature, the executive, and the judiciary as the institutions required for limited government; it constructs the separation of powers to govern the relations between the branches (notably by identifying which matters fall to each of the branches and which matters fall to none of them); and it imposes the requirement of rule governance (and all which that implies: transparency, the prohibition of retroactivity, and so on)[2] to regulate the conduct of all branches. Our current concern, however, is the fourth requirement of political morality, the matter of the extent and nature of political regulation of relationships between members of political community. For this is where the morality of the liberal state confronts the question of the limits of state authority, and this is where the substance of the separation of powers is finally forged. The rule of law's answer to these matters resides in the founding distinction between personal and political morality.

The rule of law, then, is a political morality conceived with reference to an excluded realm of personal morality. This has three consequences, which together provide the basic geography of limited government.

> The body politic is a "body" defined by the exclusion of real bodies.

First, the distinction creates a cleavage between the public and the private and between citizenship and personhood. The private is the sphere in which law and politics are disabled. And, except when it chooses to recognize (in ways to which we will come) the practices of persons, the state's proper subjects are its *citizens* and not the *persons* of those who in their capacity as citizens are the state's subjects. To put it another way, the body politic is a "body" defined by the exclusion of real bodies.

Second, the excluded realm of personal morality gives structure to the relationship between political and private life. Traditionally, Western cultures are "culture[s] of the social, not the political," because the purpose of the political, of limited government, is to save safe the social from the political.[3] Thus arrives the happy paradox of liberal law and politics: the political is at once marginal to, and critical for, the social. Or, as put so much better by Llewellyn: "Law means so pitifully little to life. Life is so terrifyingly dependent upon law."[4]

Finally, included in the politically excluded realm of private life are the traditions and institutions that individuals, as persons and not as citizens, have over the wealth of time accreted as visions and means of the good life, and through which they have exercised sovereignty over their lives. It is indeed true, then, that "the customs . . . of a free people are part of their liberty."[5] Liberal politics knows those customs, traditions, and institutions collectively as civil society, and civil society may therefore be said to be a normative corollary of liberal political morality.

The principles that ground the way of life promised by limited government flow from these three consequences. That way of life is distinguished first of all by the priority of persons.[6] State and law exist for the sake of persons; persons, even when they take on the mask of citizenship, do not exist for the sake of the state and law.[7] Personhood, then, is prior and superior to citizenship, and because it is, persons, in the view of liberal law and politics, constitute themselves not in their relations with the state but through their interactions with each other beyond the state.

State and law exist for the sake of persons; persons, even when they take on the mask of citizenship, do not exist for sake of the state and law.

This priority implicates a second, the primacy of the social over the political. If state and law are for the sake of persons and if personhood is an accomplishment of social interaction, then the social is prior, and superior, to the political.

Civil society, as noted, is the realm of the social; in the liberal view, the state, consequently, is parasitic on civil society. This dependence takes two forms. First, because it is there alone that persons exist, civil society is the source of a moral equality beyond identity and difference, an equality that is the foundational norm of our law and politics and that alone supplies motive and content to legal equality. Second, the rights that take shape in the rule of law rely on, because they are meant to reflect and to protect, the prior, natural "rights of ordinary life."[8]

The priority of persons and the primacy of the social together raise the third principle of the way of life of limited government. This principle concerns the constitutive tasks – or perhaps better put, the constitution – of the liberal democratic state. There are two. First, the liberal state is pledged to maintain the primacy and the autonomy of civil society. From this pledge two common features of liberal governance arise: the prohibition against totalitarianism (or state occupation of the private sphere through legal imperialism) and, with that, the commitment, institutionalized through the rule of law, to limited government. Second, the liberal state is pledged to maintain the separation between matters and values public and private. From this pledge in turn arises the prohibition against sectarianism in public life and policy and, with that, the commitment to institutional formalism generally and to formal equality specifically.

Civil Society and Liberal State

In what ways, given the principles above, may a liberal state properly relate to civil society?

Civil society is "the culture of daily life,"[9] and, certain exceptions aside,[10] it is through the preservation of that culture that the liberal state makes good its central and defining promise: that its subjects will, as persons, be left alone to author their so-brief lives as each sees fit, provided only that they cause no one harm. Leaving its subjects alone in this fashion does not, however, preclude the liberal state from addressing the institutions and practices of civil society. But if it does choose to address, through law and policy, the ways of life of its subjects, it must do so in a manner that defers to the moral and political primacy of social life, thus acknowledging the limits of its own authority. The liberal state may only speak in these ways when the law and policies through which it addresses civil society have as their aim the recognition of its institutions or practices. To recognize is to preserve and thus to enforce the importance of an institution or practice to the way of life of the persons who are the subjects of the state's laws and policies. Recognition, through law, is, then, another way the liberal state honours the self-ownership of the legal subject and acknowledges the sovereignty over the good of which its subjects are, by force of constitutive principle, seized.

The reformation of social institutions, traditions, and practices is beyond the authority of a liberal state.

The exceptions previously noted aside, the reformation of social institutions, traditions, and practices is beyond the authority of a liberal state. When a state acts to reform, it seeks to replace the values and ways of living of its subjects with its own view of human life properly guided and lived. But the liberal state can neither formulate, nor proceed from, any such views. When it adopts and acts on any view of the good life, it denies the self-ownership of its subjects and their sovereignty over their lives. Consequently, it violates the political morality by which it alone is constituted and governed.

The Canadian State and the Institution of Marriage

The Canadian state – first through the judicial branch (the high-water mark in this regard being the Ontario Court of Appeal same-sex marriage judgment in *Halpern* v. *Canada*)[11] and subsequently through the federal executive (with the executive's Supreme Court reference) – has recently claimed sovereignty over marriage. I say recently because notwithstanding the authority vested in the federal Parliament by virtue of section 91(26) of the *British North America Act*, no branch of the Canadian state, until recently, ever thought it necessary or proper to define marriage. Nor, apparently, did it occur to any previous generation of officers of the federal state that the institution and practice of marriage might be redefined and thus reconfigured by force of legislative or curial decision. As noted previously, the current reimagining of the relationship between state and marriage proceeds first from the view that marriage is a legal artefact and then from the conviction that marriage must in consequence conform to state constitutional norms as articulated by the judicial branch.

My intention here is not to criticize the overweening artifice of the judgment in *Halpern*, or the federal executive's manipulative response to it, so as to discredit directly these premises on historical and normative grounds.[12] Rather, my intention is to disclose the political and legal immorality of the consequences that follow from them. In so doing, I intend to convince that the state's claim of sovereignty over marriage by constitutional means constitutes a defiance of the rule of law, a defiance that warrants the opposition of a free people.

When a state exceeds the boundaries that define its proper relationship to civil society, when it forsakes recognition and instead takes the institutions, traditions, and practices of civil society as objects properly subject to management and reformation according to its own legislative or curial standards, that state thereby abandons its position as the protector of social life and aims instead to become its supervisor and engineer. It is of little consequence that this arrogation may proceed from perfectionist zeal or raw expansionist ambition. What does matter is the practice to which it commits the state since it is from there that the consequences that must concern us flow.

Widely conceived, the management and reformation of social life commits the state to social engineering. It is the practice of the social-engineering state to coordinate the institutions, traditions, and practices of civil society with state-articulated norms concerning which values ought to guide social life and what conduct ought to be permitted. This practice depends on a certain, precise understanding of the relationship between the state and the lived lives of its subjects.

> *Widely conceived, the management and reformation of social life commits the state to social engineering.*

First, the social-engineering state assumes that the ordinary lives of its subjects are properly subject to assessment by it and that it may, therefore, either affirm or deny their normative suitability and standing. Second, consonant with this understanding, such a state believes that the persons who are subject to the state's rule, in the whole of their lives – in their values, practices, traditions, and institutions – may properly serve as "raw material" for its normative reformation of social life.[13]

This understanding of matters changes in momentous ways the moral predicates and character of the state, the nature of its law, and the moral and legal standing of its subjects. Consider the moral predicates of the state. The self-understanding of this social-engineering state constitutes nothing less than a revolution in political morality. In the view of this state, the political is no longer secondary to, and dependent on, personhood and social life. Just the opposite. Because it stands as society's supervisor and manager, the political is not only superordinate to, but indeed, at the state's discretion, it is also constitutive of, the social. And because people's values, traditions, and institutions must conform to state norms, personhood always and in all of its aspects may be trumped by the claims of citizenship.

And consider the character of the state. No longer confined to, or by, its constitutional tasks of maintaining the primacy and autonomy of the social and the separation of the public and the private, the social-engineering state is free to occupy whatever ground of social life on which it sets its legislative or curial gaze. And it is free to do so by articulating concrete norms concerning whatever aspects of the lives of its subjects it deems proper. Indeed, it is precisely in these ways that such a state coerces private conduct and forms of life. And it is for precisely these reasons that it tends to become a totalizing state as opposed to a limited one, and a state of concrete orders as opposed to one of formal rules. To the extent that it becomes either, it ceases to be a rule-of-law state: with the first, it violates the prohibition against totalitarianism; and with the second, it abandons the distinction between public and private life and values and imposes what can only be sectarian values on the whole of life.

Alterations as fundamental as these to the state's premises and character must of course rebound on the character of its law. Because liberal law is limited, it is also both intelligible and modest. Limitation resides finally in the view, indispensable to the rule-of-law state, that law has boundaries that are natural or immanent to it as a normative enterprise. Even where power exists to declare some matter law, its legality, in the liberal view, finally depends not on empowered declaration but on the tissue of principle, tested and accreted over the wealth of generations. These principles alone make of law a reasoned human good, an authoritative claim rather than an authoritarian impulse.

Modesty attends law precisely because it is anchored in this way to the reason and goodness of the past. The officers of the rule-of-law state – legislative, judicial, and executive alike – must know that legal speech and practice have a grammar and a substance that impose on them, as a condition of faithful execution of their offices, a humility concerning the possibilities of the legal.[14] Not everything is possible, indeed most things are forbidden, simply because all speech and action must find warrant in the reason and goodness of the past.

The social-engineering state recoils from these constraints. For it, law is an instrument to impose on public and private life norms articulated by those empowered to speak them. Instrumentalism of this sort robs the law of reason. And with reason removed, so, too, is goodness. Thus does the social-engineering state explode the limits of law. Thus, in consequence, does the law become for the state, and for those unfortunates subject to its rule, transfigured from a performance of principle to a morally empty vessel into which is poured the manufacture of power.

The reformist state visits its final assault on the moral and legal standing of the subject. The subject of the social-engineering state is a vulnerable subject. The subject's values and practices, and the institutions through which it constructs its life story, are always open to state surveillance and sometimes management. When this state indeed decides, as it has now with marriage, to manage an institution to which the individual subject is attached, the subject's standing as the author of its life becomes compromised, even when it is not extinguished. This is so both because the subject becomes redacted to an addressee of state policy and because its practices then become subject to, and an expression of, state norms. It should be obvious that this subject is a morally stunted and reduced one. Where there was once a wholly autonomous private person, there is now a client of state messages concerning the proper conduct of private life. And where there was once a life freely chosen and constructed from among the ways of life alive in civil society, there is now instead a life colonized by state norms.

> Where there was once a wholly autonomous private person, there is now a client of state messages concerning the proper conduct of private life.

It should not be surprising that this moral reduction implicates a legal reduction. At liberal law, the subject is a subject of the law and not merely subject to the law. What we call legal equality elevates the legal subject from a position of mere bondage to the law to a position of entitlement with respect to law. Rights thus become the stuff of legal subjectivity. Other things being equal, each of us has a right to equal protection and application of the law. Now, the origin of this right is our natural equality. We are due, as a matter of justice, equal treatment at law precisely because we are self-owning and self-authoring beings before and beyond law and politics. Because the social-engineering state changes this predicate, it also changes the content of legal equality. In this state, the focus of equality shifts from freedom from laws that disrespect our equality and autonomy to freedom to occupy state-approved forms of life. And with this, the legal subject becomes, once again, defined by its bondage to law, and the state becomes, once again, the source, and not just the custodian, of rights and duties in every aspect of its subjects' lives, public and private.

A Deeply Committed State

These consequences are at once revolutionary and atavistic. On the one hand, they constitute a rejection, very nearly root and branch, of the morality and practice of limited, rule-of-law governance. On the other hand, they are a prescription for a return to an ancien régime in which personhood and citizenship become one and in which, in consequence, the sovereign becomes the source of rights and duties, both public and private. The Canadian state's claim of sovereignty over marriage carries all of these consequences, and it must, therefore, be considered both a rejection of our political patrimony and a prescription for an atavistic form of political and personal life. Indeed, the state's claim over marriage is most egregious in these regards, because marriage is both so intimate a form of social life and the form of life through which so many claim authorship over their lives.

Neither the sincerity of the social-engineering state as regards its reformist projects, nor the values for which it acts, changes any of this. The social-engineering state is a deeply committed state. Its officers, especially those of the judicial branch, spearhead this commitment. They sincerely believe that, when and where social life can be shown to violate state norms, the task of redeeming the social, for the sake of the better conduct of life, falls unavoidably to them. This aspiration and motive make the officers of the reformist state certain of their ends and blind to and careless about the consequences of their decisions.

In the contemporary period, equality, not imperialism, is the value on which the social-engineering state acts. "Equality" degrades this already harmful ethic of conviction into a practice of disrespect. Those who stand against the projects of the reformist state come to be viewed by its officers as standing for inequality. This is why they give so little respect to those who dissent in the name of limited government and in defence of civil society: the dissenters deserve no respect because their position violates the deeply held and incontestable norm of equality. Perhaps more than anything else, this intolerance will be the acid by which the social will be completely corroded by the political.

Those who stand against the projects of the reformist state come to be viewed by its officers as standing for inequality.

Dancing to the State's Tune

The post-liberal Western state has, for some time, been laying siege to social and personal life. Yet the nature of the present assault is no different from previous assaults. Like earlier regimes, communist and other, that were similarly engorged with commitment and inflated with power, contemporary states seek to manage social and personal life by making both dance to the state's tune of human life properly and well lived.[15] And as did they, contemporary states orchestrate this achievement by extending their normative reach and by differentiating and dividing political and legal subjectivity. That, under present circumstances, the judicial branch, rather than either of the other two branches, is the medium of these practices will, I think, come to be viewed as one of the great ironies of the Western legal tradition.

From one vantage point, of course, the Canadian state is but a local performance of this phenomenon. In the particulars of its performance, however, the Canadian state, led by its judicial branch, may be fairly judged to be an especially committed and adept managerial state. Nowhere else has political and legal fellowship been so divided. Nowhere else has the conquest of ordinary life been undertaken with such high-mindedness. The apotheosis of the latter has arrived with the state's conquest of marriage. For this conquest threatens to destroy ways of being that are most basic both to the conduct of autonomous personal life and to the preservation of political liberty.

Notes

1 Thomas Nagel, "Ruthlessness in Public Life" in Stuart Hampshire, ed., *Public and Private Morality* (Cambridge: Cambridge University Press, 1978), p. 90.

2 Concerning which, see Lon L. Fuller, *The Morality of Law*, rev. ed. (New Haven, CT: Yale University Press, 1964).

3 John Rawls, *Political Liberalism* (New York: Columbia University Press, 1993), p. 14.

4 Karl N. Llewellyn, "What Price Contract? – An Essay on Perspective" (1931), *Yale Law Journal* 40: 751.

5 Charles L. DeS. Montesquieu, *The Spirit of the Laws*, trans. Anne M. Cohler, Basia Carolyn Miller, and Harold Samuel Thorne (Cambridge: Cambridge University Press, 1989), p. 325.

6 For an excellent account of this primacy, see John Finnis, "The Priority of Persons" in Jeremy Horder, ed., *Oxford Essays in Jurisprudence* (Oxford: Oxford University Press, 2000), p. 1.

7 Larry Siedentop, *Democracy in Europe* (New York: Columbia University Press, 2001), pp. 51–61.

8 Alberto Melucci, "Social Movements and the Democratization of Everyday Life" in John Keane, ed., *Civil Society and the State* (London: Verso, 1988), p. 258.

9 Rawls, op. cit.

10 There are two exceptions only to the rule of preserving social life: first, where a standing institution of social life is perniciously opposed to and, therefore, corrosive of, the moral equality and social and political liberty for the sake of which the liberal state exists; and second, where the inequality exhibited by an institution has, in whole or in part, been created by past state excesses. The paradigmatic and perhaps the sole example of the former is slavery, and of the second, the construction at common law of equality- and liberty-diminishing legal and thus social identities for women. In the former instance, the liberal state has a positive obligation to abolish the institution; and in the latter instance, it has a positive obligation to correct the legal and social consequences of its excess and, with that, to reform the institution. I might add here that the law's construction of the subordinated identity "homosexual" is another example of the second which, as in the case of women, visited on the liberal state the obligation to cleanse social relations of the inequality that its laws wrought.

11 (2003) O.A.C. 172 [hereinafter *Halpern*].

12 Concerning both of which, see F.C. DeCoste, "The *Halpern* Transformation: Same-Sex Marriage, Civil Society, and the Limits of Liberal Law" in *Alberta Law Review* 41.2 (2003): 619.

13 Jon Alexander and Joachim K.H.W. Schmidt, "Introduction: Social Engineering" in Adam Podgorecki, Jon Alexander, and Rob Schields, eds., *Social Engineering* (Ottawa: Carleton University Press, 1996), p. 1.

14 For an account of the decline of humility and the rise of a social-engineering ethos in the legal community, see Michael P. Schutt, "Oliver Wendell Holmes and the Decline of the American Lawyer: Social Engineering, Religion, and the Search for Professional Identity" in *Rutgers Law Journal* (1998): 143.

15 For an illuminating meditation contemporaneous to those earlier experiments in state expansionism, see Arthur Liebert, "Political Morality" in *Ethics* 49.1 (1938): 62 (trans. S.C. Steinbrenner).

FOUR
The Alternative

TAKING SECTION 33 SERIOUSLY
Taking Section 33 Seriously

F.L. (Ted) Morton

In his 1890 classic, *The Law of the Constitution*, A.V.C. Dicey, the most famous British jurist of the nineteenth century, explains the concept of parliamentary supremacy thus: "Parliament can do everything but make a woman a man, and a man a woman."

Dicey would be surprised if he could witness how Canadian courts, a century later, have surpassed the abilities of his beloved parliament. Armed with the *Canadian Charter of Rights and Freedoms*, our judges believe they can repeal the laws of nature. This is the gist of the three provincial appeal court rulings (British Columbia, Ontario, and Québec) that Canada's definition of marriage as applying only to a man and a woman is unconstitutional. According to the judges, this traditional (and universal) definition of marriage violates the *Charter* right to equality of homosexual couples who want to marry.

Now, if the *Charter* explicitly guaranteed to homosexual couples the identical rights enjoyed by heterosexual couples, those of us who think same-sex marriage is a massive social experiment with unknown consequences would have no basis for criticizing these judges. The judges would simply be doing their duty: enforcing a constitutional rule. But nothing could be further from the truth. Not only does sexual orientation not appear

> *The judges would simply be doing their duty: enforcing a constitutional rule. But nothing could be further from the truth.*

in the equality-rights section of the *Charter*, but a motion to include it was explicitly rejected by those who framed the *Charter*. The judges have brazenly put in what the framers kept out.

Sensing the weakness of this original position, the Court and its defenders are quick to invoke the "Constitution as a living tree" metaphor, claiming that they are just "updating" the meaning of equality to keep pace with changing public opinion. This claim is even more fraudulent than the first. Are we to believe that the super-elite, institutionally insulated world of appeal-court judges is more in tune with "changing public opinion" than elected legislators who must go to the people every three to five years to keep their jobs? The pretence that judges, drawn from the effete lawyering class (one-tenth of 1% of Canadians), unelected and appointed for life, are an accurate measure of changing public opinion, verges on farce. The checkout line at Canadian Tire on Saturday morning would be more accurate.

And you don't have to be Angus Reid to predict what their verdict on gay marriage would be, which is why gay-advocacy groups like EGALE (Equality for Gays and Lesbians Everywhere) and LEAF (Legal Education and Action Fund) are in the courts so often in the first place. They know that they cannot achieve what they want (as fast as they want) through the democratic process. They are using the courts to change public opinion, not reflect it.

The final and highest-toned defence of court-ordered gay marriage is the appeal to human rights. But since when was homosexual marriage a human right? Is it listed in the U.S. *Bill of Rights*? The 1948 *United Nations Declaration of Human Rights*? The *European Declaration of Human Rights and Freedoms*? The 1960 Canadian *Bill of Rights*? The 1982 *Canadian Charter of Rights and Freedoms*? The *Meech Lake* (1987) or *Charlottetown* (1992) Accords? Is it a recognized right in any Western democracies other than Holland and Belgium? How about the other 160-odd countries in the world?

The answer to all of the above is no. In Canada, the idea that homosexual marriage is a right is a judge-made affair from start to finish. Even this is new, since the Supreme Court of Canada's 1999 homosexual rights ruling – *M* v. *H*,[1] in which it extended common-law spousal rights to homosexual couples – explicitly declared that this ruling did not affect or address the issue of marriage.

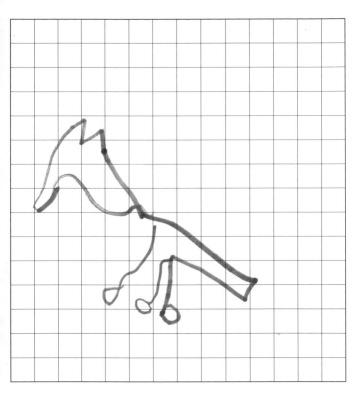

Gilmore
Printing Services Inc

110 Herzberg Road, Kanata, Ontario K2K 3B7
Tel: (613) 599-3776   Fax: (613) 271-1332

So what has changed since 1999? How did homosexual marriage suddenly become a human right? Because its advocates say it is. This is the new game of *Charter* politics: take your favourite policy issue, dress it up as a human right, and take it to court – preferably with taxpayers' money from the federal Court Challenges Program. Not only has this trivialized the whole notion of rights (Is there anything left that isn't a right?), but it also has dealt a severe blow to democracy. The moment something is declared a fundamental human right, any opposition to it is stigmatized. Democratic debate is at an end. This is not constitutional supremacy. It is judicial supremacy. The academic and media elites' embrace and defence of this new form of jurocracy shows that Canada's democratic deficit is not limited to governments.

> *This is the new game of Charter politics: take your favourite policy issue, dress it up as a human right, and take it to court.*

Section 33 in History and in Theory

The failure to check this type of excessive judicial activism under the *Charter* is surprising, because the Canadian framers anticipated this problem and provided a direct remedy: the section 33 notwithstanding power. Section 33 of the *Charter* allows a government, federal or provincial, to protect its legislation from judicial review under sections 2 (fundamental freedoms), 7–14 (legal rights), and 15 (equality rights). To do this, a government must insert a clause in the contested piece of legislation declaring that it "shall operate notwithstanding" any provisions of the *Charter*. The use of section 33 is limited by a five-year sunset clause, at which time it ceases to have any legal effect. Alternatively, it may be renewed for another five-year period. Since it was intended to serve as an instrument for legislatures to respond to incorrect or unacceptable judicial decisions, it is also commonly referred to as the "legislative override" power or as "opting out."

Section 33 was one of the compromises worked out between former Prime Minister Trudeau and seven of the eight provinces that opposed his "constitutional patriation" plans in 1980–81. Eight provinces (all but Ontario and New Brunswick) opposed Trudeau's proposed *Charter* because it transferred so much power to judges, especially the Supreme

Court. They thought that this empowerment of the judiciary conflicted with Canada's longstanding tradition of parliamentary democracy and that it would undermine the capacity of the provinces to be self-governing. They feared that federally appointed superior-court judges would use the *Charter* to unfairly strike down provincial policies.

Their acceptance of the *Charter* in November 1981 was conditional on Trudeau's acceptance of the legislative override power. As described by former Alberta Premier Peter Lougheed, "The final 'deal' on November 5, 1981 was, as is almost always the case, a trade-off. Essentially Mr. Trudeau got his *Charter* and the Western Premiers got both the Alberta Amending Formula and a notwithstanding clause."[2] Without the notwithstanding clause, there would be no *Charter*.

The notwithstanding device was not new. A similar clause was part of the 1960 Diefenbaker *Canadian Bill of Rights*. When the newly elected Alberta Tories took office in 1972, they enacted a provincial *Bill of Rights* that included a notwithstanding clause. Similarly, the *Québec Charter of Human Rights* and *Saskatchewan Human Rights Code* also contained such a clause prior to the adoption of the *Charter*. Because of his personal familiarity with the notwithstanding device, Lougheed took the lead, suggesting it as a way to break the federal-provincial deadlock over the proposed *Charter* in 1980–81. As Lougheed later explained: "The then Premiers of Manitoba and Saskatchewan and the Premier of Alberta took the position in the constitutional discussions that we needed to have the supremacy of the legislatures over the courts . . . We did not [want] to be in a position where public policy was being dictated or determined by non-elected people."[3]

Contrary to critics, section 33 was not a right-wing conspiracy. The then NDP premier of Saskatchewan, Allan Blakeney, was even more adamant than Lougheed about including an override provision. Blakeney successfully insisted on other changes in the wording of the *Charter* to pre-empt judicial activism. Looking back, in a 1997 interview, Blakeney explained, "I had real reservations about a constitutional *Charter of Rights and Freedoms*, because of its ongoing tendency to have the courts heavily involved in decisions which are essentially political and hence [bring] about a politicization of the courts."[4]

Nor was the Liberal government all that opposed to section 33, since it gave the federal government the same power, something that its provincial supporters had not demanded. When Trudeau's then justice minister, Jean Chrétien, introduced the amendments in the House of Commons on 20 November 1981, he defended section 33 on principle, not just as a "necessary evil." Section 33, Chrétien explained, would serve as a "safety valve" to ensure "that legislatures rather than judges would have the final say on important matters of public policy." According to Chrétien, section 33 would allow elected governments "to correct absurd situations without going through the difficulty of obtaining constitutional amendments."[5]

Commenting at the time of the November 1981 compromise, Alan Borovoy, founder and long-time Executive Counsel of the Canadian Civil Liberties Association, assessed section 33 in glowing tones: "Canada at the moment is a parliamentary democracy in which the will of Parliament is supreme. If there were no notwithstandings in the proposed Constitution, this supremacy would shift to the judges who would decide whether or not a law offended the Constitution . . . By making it legally possible but politically difficult to override the *Charter*, they have married the two notions . . . The result is a strong *Charter* with an escape valve for the legislatures."Since then, academic commentators have provided a variety of descriptions of section 33 that capture its attempt to balance the power of accountable governments and non-elected judges. Professor Paul Sniderman of Stanford University elaborates on this in a book published by Yale University Press in 1996:

> The root issue is who shall have the final word: the courts in their role as ultimate authorities on the *Charter*, or the parliaments, in their role as ultimate representatives of the public? Regimes following the American model have invested final decision-making power in courts; regimes following the English model have put it in Parliament. What distinguishes the Canadian regime is its deliberate effort to forestall an authoritative answer to the question of who shall have the final word. The Canadian political order invests final institutional power simultaneously in the courts, above all the Supreme Court, and in parliaments, both federal and provincial.[6]

While it has since become stylish to dismiss the notwithstanding clause as an unfortunate concession, no less an authority on constitutional matters than Professor Peter Russell of the University of Toronto has given it high marks: "The override gave Canada an opportunity to get the best out of British and American constitutionalism . . . to strike a shrewd balance between the wisdom derived from these two parts of our heritage . . . The *Charter* . . . establishes a prudent system of checks and balances which recognizes the fallibility of both courts and legislatures and gives closure to the decisions of neither."[7]

Who Gets the Last Word?

Despite such an auspicious birth, the notwithstanding clause soon fell on hard times. To protest the adoption of the *Charter* without its consent, the Québec government routinely attached the notwithstanding clause to every law it enacted between 1982 and 1985. The Québec government also applied it retroactively to all Québec laws enacted prior to 1982. Since 1986, however, the notwithstanding clause has been used only 16 times by four different provinces: the Yukon (1), Saskatchewan (1), Alberta (1), and Québec (13). As of 2001, eight instances were still in force. Almost all have been pre-emptive uses to prevent judicial review. Policy areas include back-to-work legislation, land-use planning, pension plans, education, agricultural operations, and same-sex marriage (Alberta's 2000 *Defence of Marriage Act*).

However, both federal and provincial governments have used other means to reverse or nullify judicial decisions deemed unacceptable. Alberta and Saskatchewan used normal legislation to reverse Supreme Court rulings on constitutional language rights that fall outside the *Charter*. In the case of *Mercure* v. *Saskatchewan*, the Supreme Court ruled that the *Saskatchewan Act* of 1905 obligated Saskatchewan to enact all its legislation in both French and English. The same logic applied to the *Alberta Act*. In both instances, however, the Court ruled that since this legal obligation was in the provinces' own constitutions, it could be validly repealed by the respective governments, provided that the repealing legislation was itself enacted in both official languages. The governments in both provinces chose this option and amended their laws to repeal any obligations for bilingual legislation.

While Ottawa has not yet used section 33, it has reversed more Supreme Court *Charter* decisions than any of the English-speaking provinces. In three different instances, Ottawa has enacted remedial legislation to respond to *Charter* rulings that it found politically unacceptable. In 1991, then justice minister Kim Campbell introduced Bill C-49, reversing the Supreme Court's *Seaboyer*[8] decision, which had struck down the "rape-shield" provision in section 276 of the *Criminal Code*. In 1995, then justice minister Allan Rock introduced Bill C-72, reversing the Supreme Court's 1994 *Daviault*[9] decision, which had allowed extreme intoxication a defence against otherwise criminal conduct. In 1996, Allan Rock introduced Bill C-46, reversing the Court's *O'Connor*[10] decision, which had allowed the accused access to the past medical records of the victim in sexual-assault cases. While this form of legislative reversal is not the same as employing section 33, it reaffirms the principle behind section 33: that courts can make mistakes and that in such instances they should not have the last word.

> Courts can make mistakes and in such instances they should not have the last word.

In the related field of the constitutional law of federalism, it is widely accepted that the Supreme Court does not have the last word on disputes over division of powers. Professor Russell concludes in a 1985 article that the "legal consequences" of a Supreme Court decision are not the same as its "political consequences." The latter, he observes, "are determined by the intentions and resources of politicians." In the end, Russell finds, "the level of a government's activity in a given policy field depends less on its constitutional resources than on its will to use the resources it has."[11]

Building on Russell's work, Patrick Monahan, the current dean of Osgoode Hall Law School, has proposed as a "fundamental maxim" of Canadian federalism that "contrary to repeated judicial pronouncements to the contrary, it is always possible to do indirectly what you cannot do directly."[12] He presents a series of cases studies that support this claim. For example, in 1978 when the Supreme Court struck down Saskatchewan's "windfall profits" production tax on oil, the province responded by enacting a new income tax that recovered the same amount of revenue.[13] Several years later, Premiers Blakeney and Lougheed teamed up to force Ottawa to accept a constitutional amendment that gave provinces the power to lay taxes of any sort – direct and indirect – on non-renewable natural resources. Monahan concludes that despite an initial legal loss, "in each instance, the governments concerned were able to achieve the same regulatory goals through alternative instruments." In sum, in the constitutional law of federalism, political reversal or avoidance of judicial rulings is the norm for policies that a government really cares about.

Québec's use of section 33 – primarily to restrict language rights of anglophones in that province – has given it a bad reputation in English-speaking Canada. This reputation is unmerited. The campaign in English-speaking Canada to undermine the integrity of section 33 has been carried out by the "Court Party" – those *Charter*-based interest groups and their supporters in the media and academia, who would prefer a regime of judicial supremacy.[14] However, as the preceding examples illustrate, there are numerous precedents for governments refusing to accept judicial interpretations of the Constitution as final and conclusive. Practice confers its own legitimacy.

> *There are numerous precedents for governments refusing to accept judicial interpretations of the Constitution as final and conclusive.*

What are the arguments in support of this practice as it is enshrined in the notwithstanding clause? The basic argument for section 33 is the same one that Peter Lougheed used in November 1983 to defend his government's proposed use of section 33 to prevent hospital workers from striking: "We did not [want] to be in a position where public policy was being dictated or determined by non-elected people." Ten years later, in the first Merv Leitch Memorial Lecture at the University of Calgary, Lougheed reaffirmed his support for this principle: "I hold to the same view as then. The notwithstanding clause . . . should be retained on the basis of the supremacy of the elected Parliament over an appointed judiciary."[15]

Lougheed's defence of democracy basically reasserts and reinforces the basic wisdom of U.S. President Abraham Lincoln's views on the same issue a century earlier (on which more in a moment). The case against judicial supremacy has been affirmed and elaborated by some of Canada's most distinguished constitutional scholars, including Peter Russell of the University of Toronto;[16] Paul Weiler, now at Harvard

University;[17] Christopher Manfredi of McGill University;[18] and Patrick Monahan, Osgoode Hall Law School.[19]

Beyond this basic argument, the case for the notwithstanding power has seven compelling arguments.

Section 33 Checks Judicial Fallibility

The myth of judicial infallibility must be challenged and unmasked. The Court's defenders blithely claim that the *Charter* means whatever the judges say it means. This can only mean that the *Charter* cannot be misinterpreted, or the judges are infallible. Both claims are, of course, absurd. The concept of judicial infallibility is contrary to both common sense and history. (The United States Supreme Court once ruled that African slaves were not human beings; the Supreme Court of Canada that women were not persons.) As a former Chief Justice of the United States once dryly observed, the judges are not final because they are infallible; they are infallible because they are final.

> *The concept of judicial infallibility is contrary to both common sense and history.*

Russell points out that judicial fallibility is not an argument for not having a *Charter*. Rather, it is an argument for having a backup device when judges do get it wrong: "But occasionally situations will arise in which the citizenry through a responsible and accountable process conclude that a judicial resolution of a rights issue is seriously flawed and seek to reverse it. These are the situations in which we should enjoy the benefit of the legislative override."[20] McGill's Manfredi makes the same point, saying that "elevation to a nation's highest court does not transform an individual into a moral philosopher. Indeed, there is nothing in legal training or in the practice of law that imparts superior judgment in such matters."[21]

Manfredi's point has recently been echoed by Allan Blakeney, one of the original supporters of section 33: "The courts are so ill equipped to deal with the social issues. First, it may not be in their [professional] background. But secondly, they can only consider statutes and cases. It's very difficult for them . . . to gather in all the facts about this issue, so that they will have the full range of arguments before them."[22] John Richards, author of the influential recent study *Retooling the Welfare*

State, goes even further in criticizing the capacity of judges to solve policy problems. He suggests that "a negative correlation exists between the extent of judicial review of social programs and their quality: the more review, the lower their quality."[23]

Critics of section 33 claim that it contradicts the rule of law. But as Abraham Lincoln argued in his first inaugural address, in 1861, the rule of law requires only the acquiescence of the "parties to a suit, as to the object of that suit." The rule of law does not require that elected governments passively accept a larger and more enduring constitutional (mis)interpretation of the Court. Here is what Lincoln said in explaining why he refused to accept the U.S. Supreme Court's ruling in the *Dred Scott* case that African slaves were property, not human beings:

> I do not forget the position assumed by some, that constitutional questions are to be decided by the Supreme Court; nor do I deny that such decisions must be binding in any case, upon the parties to a suit, as to the object of that suit . . . At the same time the candid citizen must confess that if the policy of the government, upon vital questions, affecting the whole people, is to be irrevocably fixed by decisions of the Supreme Court, the instant they are made, in ordinary litigation between parties, in personal actions, the people will have ceased to be their own rulers, having to that extent, practically resigned their government into the hands of that eminent tribunal.

Lincoln's distinction was reaffirmed by Justice Gérard La Forest in an interview upon his retirement from the Supreme Court of Canada in September 1997. In reference to Parliament's reversal of the Supreme Court's decisions in the area of drunkenness (*Daviault*) and sexual assault (*O'Connor*), he was asked whether he was concerned that "Parliament doesn't show enough deference to the Supreme Court." "Not a bit," he responded. Justice La Forest's response acknowledges judicial fallibility and the desirability of a shared judicial-legislative responsibility for *Charter* development: "I'm glad to see the dialogue. I don't think we or Parliament are the final repositories of wisdom. To me, it is all process. We are forever reaching out for a balance which is best for the common good. When you get to the *O'Connor* case, Parliament said that we [the minority judges] were right."[24]

Section 33 Protects Against the Non-constitutional

A second argument in support of section 33 is that actual *Charter* cases raise issues of public policy design rather than issues of fundamental justice. As Russell points out, "The kind of questions courts typically deal with in interpreting and applying a constitutional charter of rights . . . are questions not about the validity of the core values enshrined in the general language of the *Charter*, but about the proper limits of rights based on these values."[25] The "free and democratic" character of Canadian society does not hang in the balance in *Charter* cases. A survey of other Western democracies reveals a diversity of approaches on almost all policy issues raised by *Charter* cases. This is clearly the case with homosexual marriage, a policy that is still strongly rejected by an overwhelming majority of liberal democracies.

The "free and democratic" character of Canadian society does not hang in the balance in Charter cases.

Patrick Monahan endorses the override for similar reasons. Section 33, he says, does not "legitimate tyranny" but rather ensures "that the political process will not be subject to unreasonable or perverse judicial interpretations."[26] Manfredi makes much the same point: "The principal issue in an overwhelming majority of *Charter* cases is not legislative abrogation of rights, but the constitutional validity of a shifting balance in the relative importance attached to competing rights . . . Section 33 does not permit legislatures to override rights, but to override the judicial interpretation of what constitutes a reasonable balance between rights."[27]

The political character of *Charter* cases becomes evident when we look at who initiates most (non-criminal) *Charter* cases: interest groups. The rights-claiming stimulated by the *Charter* is best understood as an extension of – not an alternative to – interest-group politics. The objective of these new rights advocacy groups is not to protect rights traditionally understood but to enlist the moral authority of the right claimed as a means of persuading judges to change the policy status quo. Again, this perfectly describes the gay-marriage judicial rulings, which are the result of a carefully orchestrated campaign of *Charter* challenges – all paid for by the federal government's Court Challenges program.

The core/periphery argument received a significant new elaboration in a 1996 study of public and elite opinion toward the *Charter* led by Professor Paul Sniderman of Stanford University. Sniderman poses the paradox of rights litigation by asking: "Why do we find ourselves arguing so vehemently and so often about the very core of what we have, as participants in a democratic polity, long since presumably agreed on?"[28] That is, constitutions are supposed to articulate those core values on which there is such wide consensus that we want to put them "beyond the reach" of ordinary, day-to-day political scrapping. But if such a consensus exists, why is there so much litigation contesting the meaning of these fundamental values?

The answer is not that our consensus has dissolved, but that there is a fundamental difference between core rights and the rights claims that are taken to the courts. As Sniderman points out, "typically it is not the hard, inner consensual core of a democratic right that is at issue but its outer margins, where it comes squarely into collision with another cherished right or freedom."[29] Elsewhere, he explains that disagreements over the practical application of fundamental rights are often genuine: "Reasonable people knowledgeable about individual rights frequently disagree about what ought to be done."[30] And he concludes that "the crux of the politics of democratic rights – indeed, what makes for a politics of rights – is that rights, even fundamental rights, are intrinsically contestable."[31]

This view of the intrinsic contestability of rights-claims leads him to give high praise to section 33, which he says "calls attention unmistakably to our most fundamental theme: the inescapable and essential pluralism of values in liberal democracy."[32] "The *Charter* in its final form, then, and most specifically with the inclusion of section 33, represented an ingenious compromise between two sharply conflicting visions of governance."[33]

Section 33 Is Superior to Formal Amendment or Court Packing

In theory, the most direct way to reverse an incorrect or unacceptable Supreme Court ruling is through a formal amendment to the Constitution. In practice, this rarely works. In the U.S., the nation that has the most experience with judicial activism, more than one thousand amendments have been proposed, but only twenty-seven approved. The U.S. Constitution requires a two-thirds majority in Congress and approval by three-fourths of the states to amend the Constitution – a high threshold. The new "7/50" Canadian amending formula is equally daunting. As Paul Weiler points out, if formal amendment were the only way of reversing incorrect or unacceptable judicial decisions, "a tiny minority could hold the nation in a constitutional vice."[34]

The response in the U.S. has been to use "court packing" – the partisan use of judicial appointments by the President – to curb unpopular judicial activism. Court packing also has its problems. Like amendments, it is difficult to achieve. But when it does work, it means a total remaking of the Court based on the ideological criteria and legislative program of the President and his supporters in Congress. Such overt politicization of the Court undermines judicial independence and the public's confidence in the Court. The media circus atmosphere associated with the nominations of Judge Bork and Thomas may serve as an illustration. Court packing is thus no more satisfactory than constitutional amendment. American constitutional scholar John Agresto describes a solution to the American dilemma as follows:

> The perfect constitutional solution to the problem of interpretative finality and judicial imperialism would have been for the judiciary to possess the same legislative relationship to Congress as that which governs the executive. Just as Congress, by special majority, can override a presidential veto, a similar process could from the outset have been established to review judicial objections. To have subjected judicial "vetoes" to the same process of review as that to which the Constitution subjects presidential vetoes would have been the most unobjectionable method of combining the benefit of active judicial reasoning and scrutiny with final democratic oversight. It would have been the perfect

balancing of the principle of constitutionalism with active popular sovereignty.[35]

Agresto's "dream solution" to the American dilemma is a reality in Canada in the form of section 33. As Russell observes: "There should be some process, more reasoned than court packing and more accessible than constitutional amendment, through which the justice and wisdom of these decisions can be publicly discussed and possibly rejected. A legislative override clause provides such a process."[36]

Section 33 Facilitates Federalism and Defends Community

A fourth argument in defence of section 33 is its facilitation of federalism, and by extension, of national unity. Federalism is itself a form of minority rights, in as much as each province is a minority within the larger national population. Policies that may be popular in Metro Toronto may be unpopular in Nova Scotia or Alberta. This is why at Confederation the provinces were given "the most culturally relevant jurisdictions."[37] Federalism is thus a defence of community – the ability of regional societies to define their respective political environments in a manner that reflects and reinforces their shared culture. This is what makes each province more than just an aggregation of strangers.

Federalism is itself a form of minority rights, in as much as each province is a minority within the larger national population.

Québec has always defended respect for provincial rights – and thus, provincial differences – as essential to its self-determination within Canada. Studies have documented how the *Charter* has eroded this diversity, as judges announce new constitutional norms that must be applied uniformly in all ten provinces.[38] As Russell observes, "The *Charter* does have a centralizing effect on Canadian federalism . . . [This] may reduce the policy pluralism and diversity that many of us value in federalism."[39] As anticipated by Lougheed and the other original supporters of section 33, the override power allows each province to defend what its voters consider distinctive about their regional societies. This has been most clearly the case with Québec, but applies with equal force to the other nine provinces.

Regional diversity is as significant as other forms of diversity. Indeed, the much-touted "*Charter* diversity" is fast becoming a pseudo-diversity of court-ordered uniformity to the cultural preferences of downtown Toronto. Federalism respects and protects regional diversity and the community-building this allows. The *Charter* erodes both. Where is it written that *Charter* rights should trump provincial rights? Section 33 says just the opposite. As Sniderman observes: "The inclusion of section 33 has placed into the hands of the provincial legislatures a substantial constitutional instrument to counterbalance the nationalizing influence of the powers given to courts under the *Charter*."[40]

The challenge is for a provincial premier to craft a compelling public rhetoric that makes the exercise of section 33 a legitimate defence of provincial rights and democratic self-government. The Supreme Court (in its *Vriend*[41] decision) and Professor Peter Hogg, the originator of the "dialogue theory," have provided some assistance by identifying the notwithstanding clause as a legitimate instrument of judicial-legislative dialogue.

Here we can learn something from former Ontario Liberal Premier Oliver Mowat's successful battle against the federal power of disallowance in the 1880s. Federal disallowance could not be tolerated, Mowat argued, because it destroyed the political liberty of provincial voters.

A Conservative ministry in Ottawa could thus use disallowance to thwart a provincial policy that the local Conservative opposition had been unable to stop:

The minority who form the Opposition in the Provincial Legislature have only to appeal to their friends, the Federal Ministry, and the prerogative of disallowance is at once used to frustrate the policy of the Provincial Ministers.

"Every one will see," Mowat concluded, "that if a war of this sort is to be carried on, responsible government is at an end." The ultimate question was "who shall govern the province – the majority or the minority? – the ministry to whom the electors have entrusted the Government, or the minority whom they refused to trust?"[42]

Judicial nullification of provincial policy is even more undemocratic and unaccountable than the old federal disallowance power. At least a prime minister who used disallowance was elected and accountable to Canadian voters at some point. Not the Supreme Court, whose members enjoy tenure until the age of seventy-five.

Section 33 Checks One-Party Domination of the Supreme Court

Indeed, until the year 2013 – which will be ten years after he left politics – Jean Chrétien's hand-picked appointees will still constitute a majority on the Supreme Court of Canada. Two of Mr. Chrétien's appointees, Justices Bastarache and Deschamps, are not scheduled to retire until 2022 and 2028, respectively, presumably long after their benefactor has died. Were the Liberals to fill the two vacancies created this year by the voluntary departures of Justices Arbour and Iacobucci, one party (which in the last several elections has averaged about 40% of the votes) would then have appointed all but one of the judges.

This kind of rule-from-the-grave, one-party domination of a country's highest constitutional court is one more indicator of Canada's democratic deficit. In most European democracies, opposition parties are allowed to appoint members to their constitutional courts in proportion to their representation in the legislative branches. These courts also have term limits for the judges – usually nine years. In the United States, the requirement of Senate confirmation checks the ability of a single president to remake the Court in his own image. In Canada, a more democratic appointment process is needed, but in the meantime the responsible use of the notwithstanding power is also part of the solution.

Section 33 Recognizes the Morality of Consent

A sixth reason to support the notwithstanding clause is that it balances the "morality of rights" with the "morality of consent." As Peter Russell reminds us, the fact of citizen participation is itself an important "process value," quite apart from whether the process yields the right answers to complex public policy issues: "Giving judges the last word, the definitive say, on issues of social and political justice is to exclude citizens from participation in the essential activity of a political community. In a democracy that aspires to government by discussion and full participation of its citizens in questions of social and political justice, court decisions should not close off further debate and decision-making in elected and publicly accountable legislatures."[43] Section 33 secures a role for democratic participation in the formulation of public policy.

Legislative control of judge-made policy can also be defended on the basis of rights theory. Noted legal theorist Jeremy Waldron has recently provided an influential rights-based critique of constitutional rights. According to Waldron, giving judges the final word on the meaning of constitutional rights is inconsistent with the most important of all rights, what he calls the "right of rights": the democratic right of ordinary people to participate in an equal manner in public decision-making. Giving judges the final say makes everyone else second-class citizens.[44]

Section 33 Is a Constitutional Check on Judicial Power

The seventh and final argument in support of the notwithstanding power is based on the principle of separation of powers. Contrary to its critics, section 33 actually is consistent with the first principle of liberal constitutionalism: "the subordination of all political power, including judicial power, to procedural and substantive constitutional rules."[45] Liberal constitutionalism assumes not just the fallibility of public officials, but also the influence of ambition. No office or person should be unchecked. "Liberal constitutionalism does not establish a judicial monopoly over the process of adapting constitutional language to changing social circumstances," Manfredi observes. "It is both unrealistic and inconsistent with liberal constitutionalism to expect judges to be self-restrained in the exercise of political power in the context of constitutional review."[46] Just as there is a need to check the abuse of legislative power, so there is a need to check the abuse of judicial power. Section 33 provides that check.

Just as there is a need to check the abuse of legislative power, so there is a need to check the abuse of judicial power.

Whom Can We Trust?

In sum, using the section 33 notwithstanding power is a perfectly legitimate response to the courts' usurpation of the legislative responsibility to make laws – in this case, the law of marriage. This is especially true in the case of homosexual marriage, as the courts have added new meaning to the *Charter* that was explicitly rejected when it was being written.

If governments are reluctant to invoke section 33 on their own authority, then the use of the notwithstanding power should be put to the people in a referendum. In cases like *Halpern*, the courts are trying to amend the original meaning of the Constitution. Two provinces – B.C. and Alberta – already require referendums to approve new amendments to the Constitution. Similarly, democracies like Australia and Switzerland and most of the U.S. states require a referendum to approve an amendment to their constitutions. Why shouldn't the same approach be used to approve – or disapprove – judge-made amendments to Canada's Constitution?

Critics of section 33 say that we cannot trust politicians to act as a check on the courts. Fine, if that's the case, give the decision to the people. Legitimize the use of the notwithstanding clause by democratizing it.[47] If we cannot trust politicians, surely we can trust the Canadian people. Or can we? The advocates of homosexual marriage don't seem to think so. Otherwise why are they always in the courts? Isn't the whole unspoken premise of this affair that the Canadian people can no longer be trusted to decide such issues? Unspoken, because it is too devastating to admit publicly.

> *The most fundamental question is: Why is government based on the consent of the governed no longer good enough?*

The most fundamental question is: Why is government based on the consent of the governed no longer good enough? Surely, whatever one's position on same-sex marriage, a decision this important should be made in a public and informed consultation with the thirty-three million Canadians who will have to live with the consequences, not by nine (or even five) unelected judges.

Notes

1 [1999] 2 S.C.R. 3.

2 Peter Lougheed, "The Merv Leitch, Q.C., Memorial Lecture, Inaugural Lecture" (20 Nov. 1991, the University of Calgary), p.10.

3 Ibid.

4 Transcript, "Interview on the *Charter of Rights and Freedoms*. Honourable Allan E. Blakeney, Premier of Saskatchewan (1971–82)"; interviewed by Professor Howard McConnell, College of Law, Saskatoon, Tuesday, 22 July 1997, p. 6.

5 *House of Commons Debates* (20 Nov. 1981) at 13042–43 (Jean Chrétien).

6 Paul Sniderman, Joseph F. Fletcher, Peter H. Russell, and Philip Tetlock, *The Clash of Rights: Liberty, Equality, and Legitimacy in Pluralist Democracy* (New Haven, CT: Yale University Press, 1996), p. 160.

7 Peter H. Russell, "Standing Up for Notwithstanding" in *Alberta Law Review* 29 (1991): 293–309.

8 *R. v. Seaboyer*, [1991] 2 S.C.R. 577.

9 *R. v. Daviault*, [1994] 3 S.C.R. 63.

10 *R. v. O'Connor*, [1995] 4 S.C.R. 411.

11 Peter H. Russell, "The Supreme Court and Federal-Provincial Relations: The Political Use of Legal Resources" in *Canadian Public Policy* 11.2 (1985): 161.

12 Patrick Monahan, *Politics and the Constitution: The Charter, Federalism and the Supreme Court of Canada* (Toronto: Carswell, 1987), chap. 10.

13 *CIGOL v. Saskatchewan* [1977] 2 S.C.R. 545, in Monahan, *Politics and the Constitution*, pp. 234–39.

14 See F.L. Morton and Rainer Knopff, *The Charter Revolution and the Court Party* (Peterborough, ON: Broadview Press, 2000).

15 Lougheed, "The Merv Leitch, Q.C., Memorial Lecture."

16 Russell, "Standing Up for Notwithstanding" in *Alberta Law Review* 29 (1991): 293–309; Peter H. Russell and Paul Weiler, "Don't Scrap Override Clause – It's a Very Canadian Solution," *Toronto Star*, 4 June 1989, p. B3.

17 Paul Weiler, "Rights and Judges in a Democracy: A New Canadian Version," *Michigan Review of Law Reform* 18.1 (1984): 70.

18 Christopher Manfredi, *Judicial Power and the Charter: Canada and the Paradox of Liberal Constitutionalism*, 2d ed. (Oxford: Oxford University Press, 2001), esp. pp. 188–95.

19 Patrick Monahan, *Politics and the Constitution: The Charter, Federalism, and the Supreme Court of Canada* (Toronto: Carswell/Methuen, 1987).

20 Peter H. Russell, "Standing Up for Notwithstanding" in *Alberta Law Review* 29:2 (1991): 293–309. Reprinted in F.L. Morton, *Law, Politics and the Judicial Process in Canada*, 3d ed. (Calgary, AB: University of Calgary Press (2002), p. 588.

21 Manfredi, *Judicial Power and the Charter*, p. 195.

22 Blakeney, "Interview," p. 7.

23 John Richards, *Retooling the Welfare State: What's Right, What's Wrong, What's to Be Done* (Toronto C.D. Howe Institute, 1997), p. 240.

24 Christin Schmitz, "Mr. Justice Gerard La Forest," *Lawyers Weekly*, 26 Sept. 1997.

25 Russell, "Standing Up for Notwithstanding," p. 476.

26 Monahan, *Politics and the Constitution*, p. 211.

27 Manfredi, *Judicial Power and the Charter*, pp. 190–91.

28 Sniderman, *Clash of Rights*, p. 52.

29 Ibid., p. 9.

30 Ibid., p. 53.

31 Ibid., p. 54.

32 Ibid., p. 8.

33 Ibid., p. 161.

34 Weiler, "Rights and Judges in a Democracy," p. 83.

35 John Agresto, *The Supreme Court and Constitutional Democracy* (Ithaca, NY: Cornell University Press, 1984), p. 134.

36 Russell, "Standing Up for Notwithstanding," p. 476.

37 Archer, Gibbins, Knopff and Pal, *Parameters of Power*, p. 79.

38 See F.L. Morton, "The Effect of the *Charter of Rights* on Canadian Federalism" in *Publius* 25:3 (Summer, 1995): 173–88.

39 Russell, "Standing Up for Notwithstanding," p. 476.

40 Sniderman, *Clash of Rights*, 161.

41 *Vriend v. Alberta* [1998] 1 S.C.R. 493.

42 Vipond, *Liberty and Community: Canadian Federalism and the Failure of the Constitution* (Albany, NY: SUNY Press, 1991), p. 80.

43 Russell, "Standing Up for Notwithstanding," p. 476.

44 Jeremy Waldron, *Law and Disagreement* (Oxford: Clarendon Press, 1999), p. 254; "A Rights-Based Critique of Constitutional Rights" in *Oxford Journal of Legal Studies* 13 (1993): 18.

45 Manfredi, *Judicial Power and the Charter*, p. 193.

46 Ibid., pp. 209, 211.

47 See Scott Reid, "Penumbras for the People: Placing Judicial Supremacy under Popular Control" in Anthony Peacock, ed., *Rethinking the Constitution: Perspectives on Canadian Constitutional Reform, Interpretation and Theory* (Toronto: Oxford University Press, 1996), p.186.

Facing Reality

Douglas Farrow

> Should the monogamian family in the distant future
> fail to answer the requirements of society . . .
> it is impossible to predict the nature of its successor.

> *– Lewis Henry Morgan*

Morgan's prescient observation is worth pausing over.[1] It is by no means obvious, in spite of the sustained attacks on the "monogamian" family in recent decades, and its general weakening, that this inherited form fails to answer the requirements of our society. Indeed, it is not at all obvious that our society can continue to flourish without the monogamous family at its core. It *is* obvious, however, that once we embark on the process of seeking a replacement for it there is no telling where we will stop. And the same may certainly be said respecting marriage itself, which lies at the core of the family.

Take the *Halpern* definition of marriage as a "union of two persons."[2] Not only is this definition new, lacking any historical or legal pedigree, it is also vague to the point of being unsustainable in public policy. Certainly we must ask many questions of it that are difficult to answer. Exactly what sort of union does it have in view? Given that the union no longer answers to a procreative norm, what marks it out as something of particular value to society, worthy of public recognition and support? Is there even a standard against which it can be measured? If it is a union based on love, how shall we define love, and is mere profession of love sufficient? Need the love, or at all events the commitment, be sexual? Sexual or otherwise, why should the union in question be a union of only two? And if a union of two, why should it continue to be exclusive? Why, for that matter, should it be for life? Such questions are not merely hypothetical. They are being put, and they will be put, not only in civil discourse but if necessary also in the courts.

As Canada prepares to adopt the *Halpern* definition and to undertake the *Halpern* experiment, it must do so without the comforting illusions of the *Halpern* court. Just as once, with respect to the regulation of divorce, some contended "that the laws are iniquitous, inhuman, and at variance with the rights of free citizens,"[3] so also now, with respect to marriage itself, some have contended that the opposite-sex stipulation is inhuman and at odds with civil rights. And already others are beginning to assert that the stipulation of two, "to the exclusion of all others," is equally inhuman and must be repealed. On Morgan's logic, or the *Halpern* logic, there can be no reason not to repeal it. If marriage is merely an evolving social construct, and if the governing principle is that "love has its rights" or that "love makes a family," who is to say that marriage (or those who desire to marry) should suffer such restrictions? Why should marriage *not* be whatever we want it to be?[4]

Friedrich Engels got the point a long time ago, before same-sex marriage became an issue, and the point holds whether or not we buy into the Marxism that determines his way of putting it:

What we can now conjecture about the way in which sexual relations will be ordered after the impending overthrow of capitalist production is mainly of a negative character, limited for the most part to what will disappear. But what will there be new? That will be answered when a new generation has grown up: a generation of men who never in their lives have known what it is to buy a woman's surrender with money or any other social instrument of power; a generation of women who have never known what it is to give themselves to a man from any other considerations than real love, or to refuse to give themselves to their lover from fear of the economic consequences. When these people are in the world, they will care precious little what anybody today thinks they ought to do; they will make their own practice and their corresponding public opinion about the practice of each individual – and that will be the end of it.[5]

Or rather that will be the end of marriage. The impending dissolution of a once fundamental social institution is the reality we must now face if we are determined to proceed down the path marked out for us by the *Halpern* court and by recent Liberal governments.

That people of high office or influence have managed to obscure this from the country, or at least from themselves, is a national scandal. Our decision about the redefinition of marriage is presented as a decision about whether to give a tiny fraction of the population access to an institution from which they have hitherto been barred – a decision of no importance to marriage as such but of importance to Canada's conscience as a nation committed to equality.[6] We have seen how fallacious and unconscionable this construal is, both in its premises and in its conclusion. In fact the decision we must take is a decision about whether or not to abandon marriage, and to reinvent it on the lines dictated by sexual self-interest. These are lines on which the institution cannot possibly sustain itself.

In redefining marriage Canada is redefining its own social structure, yet it has no clear idea what that redefinition entails or where its social experiment will lead.

In redefining marriage Canada is redefining its own social structure, yet it has no clear idea what that redefinition entails or where its social experiment will lead.

There are two fig leaves by which this double embarrassment – this unscientific experiment and poverty of responsible leadership – is commonly covered. Both are borrowed from same-sex marriage advocates, though their origins lie in the theology of ancient Israel. One is called "compassion," the other "justice." Compassion is invoked by the so-called "human face factor." With a little effort, and a bit of media spin, a human face can be put on almost anything, even (to revert to one of our main examples) the withdrawal of the support of marriage for children. Gays have children, too, we are told, and that indeed is offered as a reason for supporting same-sex marriage on compassionate grounds. But compassion without principle is no compassion at all. Like patriotism, it provides refuge for the dishonest. And the lack of principle here is readily apparent. Some homosexuals do have children, of course, but as couples – as a union of two – the children they have are never their own but always someone else's. Stable and exclusive homosexual coupling is very much the exception rather than the norm,[7] and a couple with children is the exception where such coupling occurs.[8] That is a relative matter, however. What is not relative but absolute is that homosexual coupling never produces children. To connect homosexual coupling with children's welfare, then, or with a stable environment for children, is nothing if not dishonest. It is a sign of the searing of our intellects, not to speak of our consciences, that so obvious a fact even needs to be stated. Or that, when stated, it immediately provokes a storm of indignation that clouds the adult faces in question.[9]

Justice is most often invoked by what may be called the race factor, and by the appeal to civil rights. It is said that same-sex marriage will lead us nowhere that we do not want to go, because nothing that is essentially just can possibly lead to such negative consequences as opponents of same-sex marriage envisage. This rejection of consequentialist or utilitarian reasoning is another remnant of the Judeo-Christian tradition, and admirable as far as it goes. But once again it is tainted with dishonesty. The "justice" of same-sex marriage is said to be the same justice that permitted blacks, for example, to marry whites in the overturning of anti-miscegenation laws. Here it conveniently escapes notice that rejecting same-sex marriage is not difficult to distinguish from anti-miscegenation sentiments, unless (in the circular fashion criticized in my earlier essay) we disallow the traditional view of marriage from the outset. On the traditional view, marriage is open to everyone, but precisely as a male–female bond that is in principle oriented to procreation. In that context it is possible to have a meaningful discussion about whether interracial or cross-cultural or intergenerational marriage, say, or polygamous or polyamorous or consanguineous marriage, is a good or a bad idea. It is also possible to decide that there should be laws restricting the latter and that there should *not* be laws restricting the former. All of this is at least coherent, even if some of it from time to time proves reprehensible (as in the case of anti-miscegenation laws).

What is not coherent, on the traditional definition, is talk of people "marrying" people of the same sex. And if it is not coherent, then it is not a question of justice any more than it is a question of compassion. Hence we cannot alleviate ourselves, through an appeal to justice, of the burden of responsibility for the choice we make about redefinition. Nor can we claim that we have no reason to fear the consequences of that choice.

Perhaps it is the utter inadequacy of these fig leaves to cover the embarrassment of our irresponsibility that encourages a spirit of haste, even of rebellion and lawlessness, such as broke out in San Francisco with the irregular issuing of thousands of marriage licences to same-sex couples. Be that as it may, there is a less obvious and far more pernicious kind of lawlessness with which Canadians must contend, as Ted DeCoste points out in his essay in this collection. Even the courts are capable of lawlessness; that is, of taking to themselves an authority that does not belong to them – the authority to redefine marriage. Marriage is not the creation of courts or indeed of legislatures. It existed and continues to exist in its own right, with an authority prior to and more fundamental than that of the state. Strictly speaking, the state has no mandate, then, and no conceivable source for such a mandate,[10] to redefine marriage or to invent an alternative to it. As Leo XIII put it in 1880, "The civil law can deal with and decide those matters alone which in the civil order spring from marriage, and which cannot possibly exist, as is evident, unless there be a true and lawful cause of them, that is to say, the nuptial bond."[11] In making an attempt to assert authority over marriage outside these parameters, the state pretends to a power over human life that it does not rightly possess. That is a subject to which we will return after pondering the alternatives to Canada's reckless social experiment with redefinition.

In making an attempt to assert authority over marriage outside these parameters, the state pretends to a power over human life that it does not rightly possess.

Weighing the Options

Canada stands at a crossroads. Its future is still open. It has a decision to make. In this book we have all agreed that redefining marriage

would be the worst possible decision. Agreement about the best alternative to redefinition is more difficult to achieve, naturally, and has not
been sought here. Something must be said about the alternatives, nevertheless, since it is with those alternatives that a better hope for Canada's
future lies. For simplicity's sake, I will reduce them to three, taking
each in turn and offering opinions for which no one else should be held
responsible. No attempt will be made to provide detailed explanations
of the legal forms in which they might be pursued; rather, I will seek to
show in brief their relative advantages and disadvantages, with a view
to commending one in particular. This will allow us, I hope, to clarify
further what is at stake in the country's decision.

1. Retain the traditional definition of marriage while regularizing civil unions and/or domestic partnerships as a formal alternative

The aims of this proposal are two. The first, which is common to all
three proposals, is to preserve marriage as a heterosexual institution
for the good of children and of society as a whole. The second is to recognize alternatives to married life and to accord those alternatives the
status and benefits they deserve. The marriage-plus-civil-unions option
seeks, or may seek, something like a "different-but-equal" standing for
those couples who choose marriage and those couples (heterosexual or
homosexual) who choose another form of public commitment. Adding
or substituting a "domestic-partnership" option allows for a broader
range of relationships to be recognized and supported by the state,
including relationships that are not sexually intimate.

The main strength of this proposal is that it tries to accommodate
the claim that marriage is not the only arrangement worthy of state
encouragement and support, without compromising the fact that marriage must indeed be supported precisely as an opposite-sex institution
oriented to child-bearing and child-rearing. A related strength is its
attempt to recognize, as far as possible, the equality-rights claims of
homosexuals.

Its strengths are also its weaknesses, however. First, there is a jurisdictional problem. The regulation of marriage and divorce are federal
responsibilities, whereas the regulation of other partnerships (including

civil unions) is a provincial matter. Given the inherent tensions of Canadian federalism, regularizing non-marital unions or associations on a national basis would be a process fraught with political and legal difficulties.

Second, there is a problem of distributive justice. How far should we go in assigning benefits to non-marital partnerships, and how far *can* we go without exhausting our resources? Benefits for all means, in effect, benefits for none.[12] But what criteria should we follow in deciding the kind of support, or the degree of support, offered to different forms of partnership? As the renowned Harvard legal scholar Mary Ann Glendon notes in the *Wall Street Journal*:

> The Canadian government, which is considering same-sex marriage legislation, has just realized that retroactive social-security survivor benefits alone would cost its taxpayers hundreds of millions of dollars. There is a real problem of distributive justice here. How can one justify treating same-sex households like married couples when such benefits are denied to all the people in our society who are caring for elderly or disabled relatives whom they cannot claim as family members for tax or insurance purposes? Shouldn't citizens have a chance to vote on whether they want to give homosexual unions, most of which are childless, the same benefits that society gives to married couples, most of whom have raised or are raising children?[13]

Obviously, this problem is not restricted to financial resources. There are other resources to consider, including intellectual and symbolic resources. How far should public education, for example, attempt to affirm and encourage these other social possibilities through its curricula or programs?

This already raises the third problem, the problem of equality. Few on either side of the same-sex marriage debate are happy with a "separate-but-equal" or even a "different-but-equal" solution. On the one side, the side taken by our courts, it is usually denied that separate *can* be equal, and so deep is the suspicion about this solution that it cannot be saved by substituting the word "different."[14] On the other side, especially when it is denied that marriage breaches anyone's equality

Marriage does not honour some persons above others; rather, it honours a certain form of relationship.

rights, there is no embarrassment about the special benefits attached to marriage. Marriage does not honour some persons above others; rather, it honours a certain form of relationship. Marital benefits are offered by the state to encourage relationships that produce and prepare the next generation of citizens in the best possible climate: a stable domesticity in which children are connected through mutual loving commitment to their biological parents and to their siblings. It will be admitted, of course, that many marriages are not like that; the stability, the love, the natural connections may be weakened or shattered by human failure or some tragic circumstance. It will also be admitted that happy alternatives may be found in the face of such tragedies. But it will not be admitted, from the standpoint of the state – things are different with religion, of course, which may accord a higher honour to the celibate – that there is a formal alternative to marriage that is of equal value to society.[15]

If, for either reason, we cannot follow entirely the logic of proposals for distinct-yet-equal institutions, we will be less inclined to face the daunting jurisdictional and distributive-justice objections. Yet this does not preclude the possibility that provinces might find appropriate ways of supporting some domestic partnerships other than marriage, through an approach that goes not so much beyond conjugality as around it.[16] There is indeed something to be said in favour of a bestowal of limited tax benefits, for example, or of other practical advantages, on those whose relationships of care and protection alleviate the state of burdens it might otherwise have to bear. On the other hand, the difficulty of setting clear boundaries and the danger of runaway costs only escalate with the introduction of a domestic-partnerships category. Certainly nothing at all can be said in favour of a bureaucratic attempt – a sort of social "gun registry" – to regulate intimate relationships as such, a prospect raised by the ruminations of the Law Commission in its *Beyond Conjugality* report. And that is where we are sure to be led if we work from the assumption (as it does) that social life arises, not from marriage and kinship, but out of an infinitely variable nexus of autonomous personal relationships. That assumption creates a vacuum at the heart of social theory that the nanny state rushes to fill.[17]

2. Replace marriage with civil unions and/or domestic partnerships

The Law Commission speculates that a general registration scheme, by providing a variety of legal mechanisms for people to achieve their "private understandings" of relational satisfaction, "could be used to replace marriage as a legal institution." In that case, "religious marriage ceremonies would continue to exist, but they would no longer have legal consequences. Only a system of civil registration would bind two people to a range of legal rights and responsibilities, and any two people who wanted to obtain public recognition and support of their relationship could register."[18] The Commission concludes, however, that Canadians are not quite ready for this, and so opts for the interim step of legalizing same-sex marriage. Faced with that imminent prospect, some opponents of redefinition propose a variation on the long-range scheme of *Beyond Conjugality*: leave marriage to the exclusive provenance of religion, while replacing it under civil law with an open registry for "conjugal" relationships within the limits still respected by the *Halpern* court.[19] Religious marriages, however, would automatically be included in such a registry; they would continue to have legal consequences.

The strengths of this second proposal are said to be several. First, by refusing to define marriage at all, the state does not take sides in a debate that is at once civil and religious; it thus respects religious decisions in their own right and in their own sphere. Second, by including religious marriages (heterosexual or homosexual) in its civil registry, it continues to allow that religious decisions have public consequences; religion is not strictly irrelevant in the public sphere.[20] Third, while withdrawing from direct engagement with marriage as a basically religious institution, the state's existing marriage and divorce regulations, suitably amended, can continue to operate (on an opt-in basis) for the protection of the vulnerable.

A number of things must be said in response, however. First, the jurisdictional and distributive-justice problems apply here, too, and are equally difficult to overcome. Second, religious liberty does appear to be bought at the price of religion's political isolation, with marriage itself as the first casualty. Marriage, just because it is in part a product of religion, must be abandoned by the state. Not only would all existing marriages be declared, for state purposes, to be civil unions; from here on no one would be able to claim marriage without religious affiliation or sanction. A civil union would be their only option, which is one reason why the Law Commission – while happy enough to isolate religion – argues that the state's withdrawal from the marriage business would not find public acceptance. Third, though religion may continue to engage the public sphere by way of the examples it sets, and so to invite the state to compare over time the consequences of following one path or another, the practical result of all this – the absence of the word "marriage" from the state's vocabulary notwithstanding – is the creation of a marriage substitute.

Otherwise put, the result is difficult to distinguish from redefinition. For the purposes of the state, hence also for civil society, marriage would be bifurcated into religious and civil components, with the latter understood to be entirely free-standing. And this bifurcation would further entrench in law, as in the social habits of Canada, the non-procreative "close-personal-relationship" model as the standard interpretive form. That model would take on a normative function in education, exacerbating a conflict in the schools that is already serious.[21] The moral and social equivalence of the procreative family unit and of non-procreative coupling, whether heterosexual or homosexual, would permeate public policy at all levels, just as surely as it would under redefinition. What is that, we may wonder, if not a strictly pyrrhic victory for those who oppose redefinition?

The second proposal, like the first one, is aimed at preserving marriage. It may also represent a deeper reservation about the wisdom of bringing homosexuality into the mainstream of Canadian culture. Yet it might well do more to facilitate this than would the first proposal, while doing less to protect marriage. Might marriage actually be better protected under something more like the vision of the Law Commission? This, too, ought to be considered – only, of course, if it can be detached from the flawed anthropology that underlies *Beyond Conjugality* and is inimical both to marriage and to freedom – that is, a respectful disestablishment of marriage, without civil unions but with a voluntary registry of domestic partnerships.

This version of the proposal appears to have three advantages. First, it does not bifurcate marriage into distinct religious and civil components, or set up in the civil sphere an ersatz form of marriage lacking the true substance of marriage. Unlike civil unions, which would disappear, domestic partnerships would not qualify for state benefits on the basis of an imitation of marriage; nor then would they raise questions about group rights and the recognition of dignity. They would qualify, rather, on the basis of flexible criteria related to the public welfare. Second, it follows that it would be easier to continue to recognize the essential contribution that marriage makes to civil society. For the disestablishment of marriage need not necessarily be read as a denial of its vital social relevance, much less as an admission of its discriminatory nature; it may even be seen as a sign of respect for marriage as something prior to civil society and immune to state interference. The health of the marriage culture would be left to the people themselves, and to the support and guidance of their respective religious and cultural communities. But there would be no mandate here for the state to support or encourage alternatives to marriage, thus undermining it by way of public policy. Third, the jurisdictional problem is avoided, though the problem of establishing the requisite criteria for domestic partnerships remains, and with it the problem of distributive justice. The latter, however, are left to the provinces.[22]

Here again it must not be overlooked that, whether standing alone or alongside civil unions, domestic-partnerships legislation may prove impossibly complex and costly, not to say interfering and oppressive. Moreover, even a "respectful" disestablishment of marriage leaves the state with no formal mechanism for supporting the prima facie right of children to know and be cared for by their own natural parents. In societies where other means of support, including that of religion, is especially strong, this may not be a problem. But where it is a problem, it must not go unaddressed, and it is difficult to see how it might be addressed under the conditions of disestablishment – especially when the occasion for disestablishment is legal pressure to divorce marriage from procreation, on the grounds that it is otherwise discriminatory and unworthy of public support.

Whether standing alone or alongside civil unions, domestic-partnerships legislation may prove impossibly complex and costly, not to say interfering and oppressive.

3. Retain the traditional definition of marriage
   while leaving the provinces to decide independently,
   according to the political will of each,
   about alternative arrangements

Supporters of the first two options, but especially of the second, tend to share the assumption that Canada is stuck with whatever decision its courts finally reach. Not so with the third option. Strangely enough, in calling for maintenance of the status quo, it is the most radical of the three. It is put forward with full awareness of the fact that the Liberal government's decision not to appeal *Halpern*, but to support it by way of a reference to the Supreme Court of Canada, is likely to produce an endorsement of *Halpern* by our highest court. Be that as it may, supporters of the third option believe not only that the *Halpern* decision is badly mistaken, but also that the matters on which it is mistaken are serious enough to warrant the use of constitutional means to override the courts if necessary. And they believe that Canadians can be persuaded of that fact.

Listen again to Mary Ann Glendon, whose piece quoted from above goes on to capture in a few words some of the key concerns elaborated in this book:

If these social experiments go forward, moreover, the rights of children will be impaired. Same-sex marriage will constitute a public, official endorsement of the following extraordinary claims made by the Massachusetts judges in the *Goodridge*[23] case: that marriage is mainly an arrangement for the benefit of adults; that children do not need both a mother and a father; and that alternative family forms are just as good as a husband and wife raising kids together. It would be tragic if, just when the country is beginning to take stock of the havoc those erroneous ideas have already wrought in the lives of American children, we should now freeze them into constitutional law. That philosophy of marriage, moreover, is what our children and grandchildren will be taught in school. They will be required to discuss marriage in those terms. Ordinary words like *husband* and *wife* will be replaced by *partner* and *spouse*. In marriage-preparation and sex-education classes, children will have to be taught about homosexual sex. Parents who complain will be branded as homophobes and their children will suffer.

Religious freedom, too, is at stake. As much as one may wish to live and let live, the experience in other countries reveals that once these arrangements become law, there will be no live-and-let-live policy for those who differ. Gay-marriage proponents use the language of openness, tolerance and diversity, yet one foreseeable effect of their success will be to usher in an era of intolerance and discrimination the likes of which we have rarely seen before. Every person and every religion that disagrees will be labeled as bigoted and openly discriminated against. The ax will fall most heavily on religious persons and groups that don't go along. Religious institutions will be hit with lawsuits if they refuse to compromise their principles.

What Glendon prophesies respecting America applies equally to Canada, as the present volume shows. Allowing for differences, so does her conclusion: "Whether one is for, against or undecided about same-sex marriage, a decision this important ought to be made in the ordinary democratic way – through full public deliberation in the light of day, not by four people behind closed doors."

For that reason, Glendon supports the movement in her country for a constitutional amendment. A similar movement is under way in Canada. Some of us are proposing that a definitional amendment be made to section 91 of the *Constitution Act, 1867*, which lists marriage and divorce among the enumerated federal powers. The understanding of "marriage" that is already implicit there could be made explicit by adding the words: "which is the lawful union of one man and one woman to the exclusion of all others." To make the implicit explicit is a move not difficult to justify, and it would bring to a fitting close, after due debate in national and provincial parliaments, a process of deliberation open to every citizen.[24]

Whatever the fate of such movements in either country – constitutional amendments are deliberately difficult, though hardly impossible, to achieve – the important thing is to have the debate. And Canada has a simple constitutional device for ensuring that the debate is not confined to the courts. That device is the notwithstanding clause in section 33. Section 33 is not a device for evading *Charter* obligations, as some contend. Section 33, by its very existence, imposes a *Charter* obligation to see that the *Charter* itself is not used or abused to override the best interests of the people and the provinces of Canada. It is present, among other things, to secure our constitutional democracy against the most egregious effects of judicial hubris or juridical error; that is, as a counterweight to the essential independence of the judiciary, and as a safeguard against the inapposite conclusions that may result either from an ideologically unbalanced court, or from the compression of broad social issues by the specialized canons of jurisprudence.

Section 33 is not a device for evading Charter obligations, as some contend.

The third option, in my view, is the best option. Canada should neither divorce marriage nor set up new categories that compete with marriage. Canada should simply say no to redefinition and begin again to learn what it means to say yes to marriage. That would still leave the country a free hand, guided by our respective provincial parliaments according to regional character, needs, and resources, to find creative ways to deal with the social realities that support for marriage addresses only indirectly. Whether the third option really is the best, however, is not the first question here. The first question is whether the government of Canada, which unlike Canadian courts is directly responsible to the people, will do what is necessary to ensure that the people are fully engaged in Canada's dispute about marriage. Accountable government can do no less.

A Defining Moment

The path that has led Canada to the brink of a disastrous social experiment need not necessarily lead over that brink. What is needed now is a new set of bearings, based on knowledge of where we have come from and of where we mean to go. Some knowledge of our roots, of our point of departure, may be gleaned from the preamble to the 1960 *Bill of Rights*, a preamble drafted initially by Paul Martin, Sr., who was also partly responsible for the inclusion of the notwithstanding clause in the 1982 *Charter*:

The Parliament of Canada, affirming that the Canadian Nation is founded upon principles that acknowledge the supremacy of God, the dignity and worth of the human person and the position of the family in a society of free men and free institutions; Affirming also that men and institutions remain free only when freedom is founded upon respect for moral and spiritual values and the rule of law; And being desirous of enshrining these principles and the human rights and fundamental freedoms derived from them, in a *Bill of Rights* which shall reflect the respect of Parliament for its constitutional authority and which shall ensure the protection of these rights and freedoms in Canada . . .

Martin's own draft included the following sentence: "Having joined with other nations and their peoples in the universal declaration of human rights, the people of Canada hereby rededicate themselves to the principles of that charter in their human, social, political, economic and legal terms, particularly those concerning the sanctity and inviolability of the family as the fundamental unit of society, the right of the individual to participate in government and to earn a living for himself and his family."[25] From such statements it may safely be deduced that the fundamental unit of society was not deemed to be subject to state determination or manipulation, but to be entitled to state protection. Needless to say, the notion that a mere forty-two years later a Canadian court would find in the *Charter* grounds for declaring marriage discriminatory in its very definition – that is, as a heterosexual, procreative, family-oriented institution – would have struck Mr. Martin and his colleagues as absurd. More importantly, they would not have considered it within the state's competence to make such a declaration.

Knowledge of our destination is obviously more difficult. That Paul Martin, Jr., and some of his colleagues do not find such a declaration absurd makes the point well enough: Canada is now conflicted about its destination; it is not certain where it should be headed or how to get there. What is certain, and we should be certain about it, is that divorcing marriage will sever the ties to our past. That will leave us without an essential set of coordinates for determining

What is certain, and we should be certain about it, is that divorcing marriage will sever the ties to our past.

169

our bearings. Moreover, if Canada presumes to divorce marriage, or in the euphemism of the day to redefine it, Canada will also be redefining itself as the kind of state that believes itself competent so to do. That sort of state is a dangerous state, whether or not the courts prove to be its most dangerous branch.[26] It is a state that no longer acknowledges the supremacy of God – its Constitution notwithstanding – and is prepared to abuse the language of human dignity, not only to alter the position of the family in society but to alter the nature and structure of the family as such. Before that sort of state a precipice yawns. As G.K. Chesterton once said, "This triangle of truisms, of father, mother and child, cannot be destroyed; it can only destroy those civilizations which disregard it."[27]

Notes

1 It is with this quotation from Morgan's *Ancient Society: Researches in the Lines of Human Progress from Savagery, through Barbarism to Civilization* (London: Macmillan, 1877) that Engels concludes the second chapter of *Origins of the Family* (1st ed. 1884, 4th ed. 1892), which was inspired by Marx's notes on Morgan.

2 *Halpern v. Canada (A.G.)* (2003), O.A.C. 172 at para. 148.

3 Leo XIII, *Arcanum* §27; see sections 25ff.

4 Why indeed should acceptable sexual behaviour not be whatever we want it to be? Some prominent figures are today disputing even the stigmatizing and criminalizing of pedophilia, for example. See the special section entitled "Pedophilia: Concepts and Controversy" in *Archives of Sexual Behavior* 31.6, (Dec. 2002):. 465–510.

5 Engels, op. cit.

6 See, e.g., "The Case for Gay Marriage," *The Economist*, 26 Feb. 2004.

7 According to a recent study conducted in Holland, men in stable homosexual partnerships have on average eight additional partners per year, and stable partnerships last on average but one and a half years (Maria Xiridou et al., "The Contribution of Steady and Casual Partnerships to the Incidence of HIV Infection Among Homosexual Men in Amsterdam," *AIDS* 17:7, 2 May 2003). So a "stable" gay relationship – this in a country that permits same-sex marriage – amounts to living together with one partner for eighteen months, while having perhaps a dozen casual partners on the side, and then splitting up: hardly an environment for children, or an argument for same-sex marriage as a stabilizing force.

8 In North America, partnered homosexuals living with children in the household (whether the household is stable or otherwise) represent less than 0.2% of the population. In most cases the partnership in question is lesbian, the children having accompanied their mother into the new same-sex situation. For other relevant background information and statistics, see, e.g., Timothy J. Dailey, "Comparing the Lifestyles of Homosexual Couples to Married Couples" (24 March 2004: www.frc.org/get.cfm?i=IS04C02).

9 The other side of the "human-face" strategy, of course, is to demonize opponents for their putative failure of compassion and tolerance: "We've heard pontificating professors masquerading behind the absurd illusion of academic neutrality and disinterest. To them, we can only say – eloquent, peer-reviewed, footnoted intolerance is still intolerance" (Douglass and Stephen Drozdow-St. Christian, the couple sought out by the CBC for a televised wedding, who should not be denied their footnote: see www.equalmarriage.ca, 10 Feb. 2004).

10 Not even a general referendum could provide such a mandate.

11 *Arcanum* §40.

12 A distinct category limiting benefits to same-sex couples could not withstand judicial scrutiny, nor is it desirable in any case.

13 "For Better or for Worse?" *Wall Street Journal*, 25 Feb. 2004 (online).

14 As Janet Hiebert reminds us, "The Supreme Court has interpreted equality as requiring not only the equal benefit and effect of law, but also has stated that the law must confer equal dignity and respect." (In "From Equality Rights to Same-Sex Marriage – Parliament and the Courts in the Age of the Charter," *Policy Options*, Oct. 2003, online.) Margaret Somerville does not see this difficulty as insurmountable, but some do.

15 Not unless it can be shown (a) that traditional marriage is not, after all, the best context for raising children, or (b) that the state has a higher interest in rewarding couples qua couples than in rewarding couples qua parents who have such a commitment to their children – in other words, that the social good of civil unions is as great as the social good of marriage. No impartial survey of the data justifies the conclusion that either (a) or (b) is the case. For that reason, it is argued, the state should not step back from its traditional role of preferring and rewarding marriage.

16 Cf. Alberta's *Adult Interdependent Relationships Act*, which specifies such relationships according to the following rather vague criteria: sharing each other's lives; being emotionally committed; and functioning as an economic and domestic unit. Sexual intimacy is not a criterion.

17 "The Law Commission believes that governments need to pursue a more comprehensive and principled approach to the legal recognition and support of the full range of close personal relationships among adults. This requires a fundamental rethinking of the way in which governments regulate relationships . . . People want stability and certainty in their personal relationships, as in other aspects of their lives. The state must provide adequate legal structures to support the relationships that citizens develop, structures that respect the values of equality, autonomy and choice. Marriage has long been the main vehicle by which two people publicly expressed their commitment to each other and sought to ensure certainty and stability in their own and their family's relationship. But marriage

is no longer a sufficient model, given the variety of relationships that exist in Canada today. What legal frameworks can the state offer to respond to the need of all its citizens for certainty and stability in their personal relationships? . . . Registration should provide options to registrants: for example, models of predetermined rights and responsibilities reflecting a conjugal relationship or a variety of caregiving relationships." (From the Executive Summary)

18 Ibid. See chap. 4, "The Legal Organization of Personal Relationships," where it is contended that "creating a registration scheme that would permit all relationships, conjugal and other, to benefit from the characteristics of voluntariness, publicity, certainty and stability now afforded only to marriage could eliminate the need for marriage . . . This idea has many advantages. By removing the link between marriage and legal consequences, the spheres of religious and secular authority would be more clearly delineated. By establishing a civil registration scheme open to all persons in committed relationships, the state could focus more clearly and effectively on accomplishing the underlying objective currently accomplished incompletely by marriage, namely, recognizing and supporting committed personal adult relationships by facilitating an orderly regulation of their affairs."

19 The word "conjugal" is now widely misused to indicate any sexually intimate relationship involving some (more or less) public form of commitment. The present proposal, however, does not intend to be open to polygamy or polyamory, etc.

20 There would be no compulsory civil ceremony, unless a province so determined for itself, though civil ceremonies would remain available for those who desired them.

21 Julius Grey notes the common concern here: "Another argument, which has already arisen in British Columbia, is that if 'marriage' is conceded, heterosexuality must lose all its privileges. For instance, school texts, according to the logic of this argument, would be required to depict gay marriages as much as heterosexual ones. However, this is an issue that need not be decided at this point, and raising it merely complicates an already thorny issue." We can only regard this last remark as disingenuous, since the whole point of an equality-rights claim is to remove special privileges. But to the advocates of civil unions it must be pointed out that the problem will not disappear with the disappearance of the word "marriage" from the state's vocabulary. (Grey's own argument for either civil unions *or* same-sex marriage is of course different from that of those who argue for civil unions in order to argue against same-sex marriage. But then Grey seems to know what no one has been able to show: that homosexuality is "a normal manifestation of human sexuality dictated by genetics or perhaps by genetic and environmental factors that cannot be altered after early childhood." On that unstable premise he rests his entire case; see "Equality Rights versus the Right to Marriage – Toward the Path of Canadian Compromise" in *Policy Options*, Oct. 2003, online.)

22 Which means that the jurisdictional problem reappears in another form, since the differences between provinces could hardly fail to create difficulties for citizens who relocate.

23 *Goodridge* v. *Department of Public Health* No. 08860 (Mass. S.J.C. 2003).

24 The wording of the *Constitution Act* is immune from review under the *Charter*. A constitutional amendment requires the concurrence of seven provinces, representing a majority of the Canadian population.

25 Paul Martin, Sr., House of Commons, Special Committee on Human Rights and Fundamental Freedoms, Minutes of Proceedings and Evidence, no. 10, 27 July 1960, p. 593: "Before God the Canadian people, united for the common pursuit of their well-being, composed of persons of various races and religions from many nations; intent on preserving (the heritage of the past), especially that of the dignity of the individual in his rights and freedoms which have been secured through the institution of parliament and the law, desire to affirm their faith in these human rights and fundamental freedoms. Having joined with other nations and their peoples in the universal declaration of human rights, the people of Canada hereby rededicate themselves to the principles of that charter in their human, social, political, economic and legal terms, particularly those concerning the sanctity and inviolability of the family as the fundamental unit of society, the right of the individual to participate in government and to earn a living for himself and his family. The Canadian people, therefore, believe that it is meet and proper that, for the better understanding of all, the parliament of Canada declare before man and God, on behalf of the nation, those human rights, fundamental freedoms, and objects of national purpose that are within its competence so to do."

26 Cf. Robert Ivan Martin, *The Most Dangerous Branch: How the Supreme Court of Canada Has Undermined Our Law and Our Democracy* (Montreal: McGill-Queen's University Press, 2003).

27 G.K. Chesterton, *Brave New Family*, Alvaro de Silva, ed. (San Francisco: Ignatius Press, 1990), p. 223.

Conclusion

Daniel Cere

On 17 June 2003, the Canadian government issued a writ of divorce, formally declaring its intention to denounce and dissolve Canada's historic commitment to the public constitution of marriage as a conjugal union of man and woman. It rushed to embrace a new "pure-relationship" mode of marriage, heralding it as the new constitutional law of the land. This public denunciation of the conjugal meaning of marriage crystallizes into law social trends that have been eroding the institution of marriage over the past two generations.

The pattern of this erosion is reflected in the movement of the main social indicators relevant to marriage: higher divorce rates, rising cohabitation rates, higher rates of unwed child-bearing, lower marriage rates, declining birth rates, declines in marital satisfaction, and declining well-being among children. Law and public policy have been channelling marriage away from its distinctively conjugal goals of sex-bridging, generativity, caregiving, and connecting children to their mothers and fathers.

Within these broad social trends dwell very real men, women, and children who are experiencing, on a personal level, the social, psychological, and economic difficulties that accompany these patterns of decline. There are too many young couples struggling to establish a family, burdened by debt, constantly on the run, leaving their young children at daycare, working long hours, worrying whether their fragile marriage will survive the stress – or actually suffering the breakdown of their marriage. There are too many children wrestling with the trauma of divorce and feeling disconnected from one or both of their parents. There are too many young women bearing the lonely burden of single motherhood and of the poverty that often accompanies it. There are too many young people desiring marriage but trapped in a series of temporary, dysfunctional relationships. There are too many adults moving into mid-life alone, with aspirations to marriage and family thwarted by a cultural matrix that seems to stymie, rather than foster, meaningful pathways to marriage.

The current project to strip marriage of its conjugal meaning is right in synch with these trends. Driven by a moral and ideological enthusiasm, it overlooks their real human costs. And it leaves unanswered far too many questions. How will Canadian society fare when it is no longer able to offer any special recognition in law or public policy to a form of life so central to human experience and, indeed, to human reproduction? Will the transformation of marriage into a close-relationships regime continue to erode its social significance for future generations? Will marriage continue to decline as a centre of gravity for women and men seeking to form a stable life together? Will these men and women have the social and cultural supports they need to help bring children into this world and to rear a family? Will the reconstitution of marriage ratify a reproductive revolution that will kill any public commitment to maintaining relationships between children and their natural parents? Will it set in motion new developments that will open the way for further deregulations of marriage and parenthood?

Those determined to alter the public meaning of marriage admonish us to shelve such questions. In Julius Grey's words, raising them "merely complicates an already thorny issue."[1] The Brave New World in which marriage has been neutered thus begins to look more and more like one in which meaningful debate will be neutered also.

At the conclusion of a major new study on American sexual practice, the authors wisely observe that there are two basic paths to choose between, in response to what they call the "disturbing" data.[2] One is the path of compliance, the other the path of renewal. The issues we have been examining are equally disturbing, and a similar choice is pressed on us.

The Path of Compliance

The path of compliance is popular among academic experts, lawyers, and public opinion leaders. These pundits look at the data of deterioration and thoughtfully conclude that "things change." The monolithic, traditional family of the 1950s is gone, they say, and that's that. They cover their compliance with happy talk about diversity. Let's just welcome the new family pluralism, whatever shape it takes.

On a recent tour promoting her book *The Meaning of Wife*, journalist Anne Kingston was doing the usual deconstructionist dance.[3] Her new take on the word "wife" proved to be the same old mantra that's been chanted for a generation: the word has no distinct meaning; "wife" can mean whatever we want it to mean; let's neuter the concept – we can have a man-wife or a woman-wife, or whatever. Really revolutionary stuff.

At one point in her talk, Kingston took a moment to fire off a few shots at the nasty old idea of marital permanence. She threw out a rhetorical question: Who, in these postmodern times, she asked, could really see themselves living with one person, having sex with one person, for the rest of their lives? The academic grayheads in the crowd seemed duly impressed, and Kingston didn't bother to wait for a reply. But one came. In a candid, matter-of-fact tone, a young university student tossed back her response: "Sounds good to me."

The young woman, thankfully, is not a voice in the wilderness. In contrast to our educated cynics, 88% of youth still want marriage for life. The institution of marriage is still deeply embedded in the lives of ordinary Canadians. True, there are 40% divorce rates, but the great majority of Canadians still try to forge a "till death do us part" marriage. True, cohabitation rates are rising steadily, but the vast majority of Canadians (including many who are cohabiting) still point to marriage as the preferred bond. True, more and more children are born and reared outside of marriage, but marriage still provides the home for the large majority of Canadian children. In short, the culture of conjugal marriage remains a stubbornly entrenched fact of Canadian life.

> The great majority of Canadians still try to forge a "till death do us part" marriage.

So what's to be done about that, if one is a firm believer in the sanctity of "the trends"? Simple. Compliance must be cultivated, even coerced. Lawyers, judges, and politicians must get their hands on the very core of marriage. The state must do some more serious social engineering. The *Charter* must be made into an effective weapon for laying siege to unconquered territory.

Coerced change to a basic societal institution is not a pretty process. The rhetoric of freedom and tolerance that accompanies the early stages of the movement becomes more and more impatient as the upper hand is gained. Compliance must be enforced, lest the inertia of social convention frustrate the reformist vision. Ways must be found to discredit the old societal norm and to suppress dissent from the new.[4] The institution of marriage is now a victim of this political hardball. The historic understanding of marriage is denounced as discriminatory and the new understanding is touted as the only one compatible with so-called Canadian values.

The Path of Renewal

What about the other path, then, the path of renewal? Is it viable?

An encouraging analogy might be drawn from successful marriage-enrichment courses. When a husband and wife realize that their marriage is in trouble, they also have two choices before them. They can refuse to change and continue to tread the self-defeating ruts that they have stamped out for themselves. Stubborn commitment to patterns of poor communication, inattentiveness, mutual recrimination, or infidelity will reinforce the decline and lead, in all probability, to divorce. Or they can recognize that there are problems, seek help, and begin to work together to turn things around. This shared struggle to deal with serious troubles is often the way to renewal and an authentically happy marriage.

The path of renewal demands that we begin to recognize that damage has been done to our social ecology over the past few generations.

Likewise with the marriage culture as such. The path of renewal demands that we begin to recognize that damage has been done to our social ecology over the past few generations. The path of renewal requires a growing commitment to the culture of marriage in our own lives, in our local communities or faith traditions, and in our political choices.

When Canadians participate in politics, and make their politicians accountable, good things begin to happen. When Tommy Douglas saw the struggle of ordinary Canadian families with rigidly privatized heath care systems, he didn't shrug and soberly dismiss, as a pipe dream, the shared hope of ordinary Canadians for public health care. The powers that be (including the Liberal Party of Canada) didn't particularly like the idea. In fact, they were rather annoyed. But Canadians began to push and push. And it happened – one of the great political achievements of twentieth-century Canadian politics.

Marriage, even more than health care, is a fundamental social good. In *The Case for Marriage*, Linda Waite and Maggie Gallagher spell out the impressive body of social-scientific evidence that underscores the social, psychological, sexual, financial, and physical benefits of a healthy marriage culture for children and adults.[5] The push for the ongoing deregulation of marriage, its reduction to a close-relationship regime, may serve the interests of a few postmodern folk. It's not a project that serves the well-being of ordinary citizens or their children. When we see current political trends eroding our public heath care, do we counsel compliance? When we see major deteriorations of the natural environment, do we just shrug and say that it's inevitable, that there's no point in fighting it? Of course not. Why, then, would we treat our hurting marriage ecology that way?

But can Canadians really hope to achieve a renewal of the marriage culture? Can we do so in a way that affirms the fundamental dignity of persons who choose paths other than marriage? Not according to many of our so-called experts, who on our national networks wag their fingers, shake their heads, and discourage us from thinking about such things. The trends are the trends. Just learn to accept them. But there's more to Canada than the talking heads would suggest. Sitting in living rooms across the country are salt-of-the-earth Canadians, tossing tidbits of satire back at the screen as they hit their remote control buttons and head to bed. There are certain things in life that can be left in the hands of media pundits. Marriage is not one of them. We need to put some confidence in the deep reservoir of wisdom in the homes of our nation, a wisdom that rarely gets air time.

We need to put some confidence in the deep reservoir of wisdom in the homes of our nation, a wisdom that rarely gets air time.

After all the ideological hype and social engineering of the last few decades, precise polling tells us that 67% of Canadians still want to see the existing definition of marriage maintained. This stubborn commitment to the common good of marriage brings together a broad spectrum of communities that make up the richness of our society. Aboriginal communities, a wide variety of other diverse ethnic and religious communities, and even some nonconforming gays (as the present volume witnesses) form a rainbow of support for traditional marriage that transcends lesser political allegiances.[6] These are people who support the fundamental dignity and equality of every human being, whatever their sexual orientation, and reject the malicious slander of those who try to claim otherwise. They are convinced that respect for persons of diverse sexual orientation and commitment to the historic meaning of marriage are not antithetical.

This preponderance of goodwill and common sense notwithstanding, we must not underestimate the challenge ahead. The task of renewing marriage in the twenty-first century is one that must be tackled on many fronts: in our homes, in our neighbourhoods, in our workplaces, in our schools, in our academies, in our places of worship, in our courts, and in our provincial and federal legislatures. Building a healthy and vibrant marriage culture for the next generation will require the collaboration of citizens, couples, parents, marriage educators, youth workers, pastors, scholars, counsellors, family lawyers, and politicians. A healthy dose of Canadian perseverance and courage will be needed. The good folk of the Shire, in whom our tradition of patience, politeness, and respect for others largely resides, must be roused to take up this challenge.

Notes

1 Julius Grey, "Equality Rights Versus the Right to Marriage: Toward the Path of Canadian Compromise" in *Policy Options* (Oct. 2003): 33.

2 Stephen Ellington, Jenna Mahay, Anthony Paik, and Edward O. Laumann, "The Cultural Economy of Urban Sexuality" in *The Sexual Organization of the City*, Edward O. Laumann, Stephen Ellington, Jenna Mahay, Anthony Paik, and Yoosik Youm, eds. (Chicago: University of Chicago Press, 2004), pp. 358–59.

3 Anne Kingston, *The Meaning of Wife* (Toronto: HarperCollins Canada, 2004).

4 Jack Knight and Jean Ensminger, "Conflict over Changing Social Norms: Bargaining, Ideology, and Enforcement" in Mary C. Brinton and Victor Nee, eds. *The New Institutionalism in Sociology* (New York: Russell Sage Foundation, 1998), pp. 105–26.

5 Linda J. Waite and Maggie Gallagher, *The Case for Marriage* (New York: Doubleday, 2000).

6 Note the diverse nature of the coalition that was pulled together, in just twenty-four hours, to issue the *Statement on the Status of Marriage in Canada*, which appeared on the *Globe and Mail* website on 18 June 2003 (see www.marriageinstitute.ca). The "marriage movement" in the United States also brings together a very broad coalition of political viewpoints, professional expertise, and civic associations. See *The Marriage Movement: A Statement of Principles* (2000, www.marriagemovement.org).

Contributors

Janet Epp Buckingham
Director, Law and Public Policy (EFC), Ottawa

Daniel Cere
Director, Institute for the Study of Marriage, Law & Culture, Montreal

F. C. DeCoste
Professor, Faculty of Law, University of Alberta

Douglas Farrow
Associate Professor of Christian Thought, McGill University

Maggie Gallagher
Co-author of The Case for Marriage *and syndicated columnist*

John McKay, MP, PC
Parliamentary Secretary for Finance

F. L. (Ted) Morton
Professor of Political Science, University of Calgary

Paul Nathanson
Researcher, Faculty of Religious Studies, McGill University

Darrel Reid
President, Focus on the Family, Canada

Margaret Somerville
Samuel Gale Professor of Law and Professor, Faculty of Medicine, McGill University

Katherine K. Young
James McGill Professor and Professor of Religious Studies, McGill University

Index